UNLIKELY BROTHERHOOD

Jan. 11, 2019

Tom,

Something unique
is going on here in
Portland, The whitest
big city in america.
    I'm certainly impressed
w/ the 20th year relationship
these two men have
developed. I hope you
like their story!

Ken

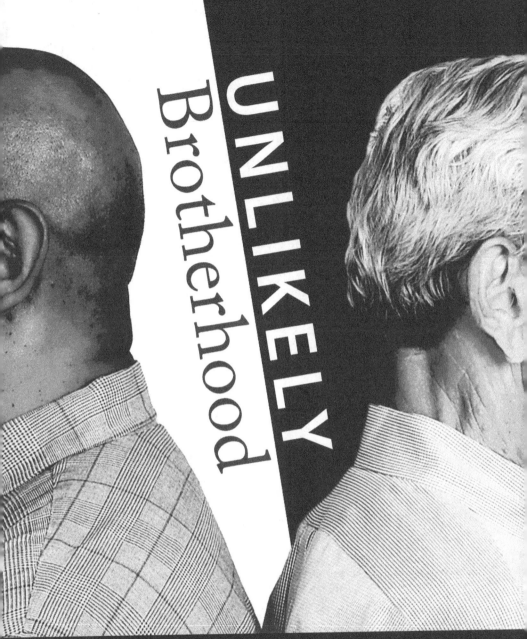

UNLIKELY
Brotherhood

LARRY ANDERSON   WENDELL BIRKLAND

with Ken Koopman

ROSE RANCH
PUBLISHING

Publisher: Rose Ranch Publishing LLC

Paperback ISBN-13 978-1-7335132-0-3 | ISBN-10 1-7335132-0-5
Hardback ISBN-13 978-1-7335132-1-0 | ISBN-10 1-7335132-1-3
eBook   ISBN-13 978-1-7335132-2-7 | ISBN-10 1-7335132-2-1

3 5 7 9 10 8 6 4 2

To Richard Twiss, our friend

CONTENTS

PART THREE
UNITED

A Rude Awakening

I knew the day wouldn't end well when I heard the two gunshots outside my second-story bedroom window. It was six-thirty on a Sunday morning, a very inconvenient time to jolt me and my family out of bed. I saw him when I got to the window—a white guy walking up my street holding what looked to me like a gun. I figured he had fired the two shots, so I grabbed my phone and called 911 to report we had an emergency situation here with shots fired. For a split second I flashed back to my days as a Portland cop— the adrenaline of facing an active shooter washed over me as I saw a police car screech to a halt across the street and then heard two armed officers shouting at the guy: *"Put the gun down! Put your hands up!"*

It was a standoff for several minutes as more police cars arrived and more officers started to mobilize. So I'm thinking they're confronting this guy, and I'm seriously expecting to witness a gun fight in front of my house. I'm watching this develop—there were about a dozen officers there by now and it looked like they were setting up some kind of perimeter. The officers were still pointing their guns and yelling at him to stop, but the guy just turned and walked away. And disappeared! I couldn't believe it. I figured the cops had him contained and they were just trying to negotiate with him so

1

they wouldn't have to shoot his dumb ass. But he was gone! About five or six minutes later, my neighbor from across the street yells down from his second-floor balcony that the guy was back in front of my property. Apparently, the man with the gun had walked around the block and was now hunkering down behind my boat, which was parked on the street with my SUV. Then all hell broke loose. I heard about twenty to twenty-five gunshots and bullets were flying everywhere. I've fired enough guns to realize bullets can ricochet just about anywhere, so at that point I grabbed my daughter and we ran downstairs to the basement.

After a while I didn't hear any more shooting, so I went back upstairs and saw the police converging on my boat. I'm thinking the guy's down on the street and they're just being careful to apprehend him, making sure he ain't playing possum or something. I had no idea the guy wasn't even there anymore! My other neighbor, who could see everything, told me she saw the shooting and then watched the guy get up from behind my boat and walk out into the line of fire. He walks right in front of the officers—there were probably a dozen of them not more than fifteen feet away—and stops at my big maple tree on the corner. Then he kind of leans up against the tree and just pauses there for a moment. She thought he had been shot because he was kind of limping. Then he just walks away. They don't shoot him; they don't even pursue him.

And for the next ten hours we had to stay in the house on lockdown while they searched for him. It was a harrowing experience, not knowing if he's got somebody hostage, if he's dead in somebody's backyard, or what. All day we were confined indoors while about fifty officers, two armored vehicles, K-9 units, and a helicopter looked for the guy. At one point I peeked out my bedroom window and saw a sniper in one of the armored trucks—his rifle pointed directly at me. In my backyard officers with machine guns were searching every corner of my property.

They eventually found a fake pistol by my boat, but they never apprehended the guy who left it there. Turns out the two gunshots I first heard were police firing their shotguns at him, but the only thing they hit was the front of a neighbor's house. Later that evening, a man who fit the description was picked up at a bus stop about a mile away. But after the authorities questioned him he was released with no charges. *Are you kidding me?* Back in my day he would have been dead or in custody. And I can tell you with all certainty in today's racially charged climate, had he been black they would have made sure he was dead. If it had been me or one of my relatives, we would have never made it out of there alive. We've heard about cops mistaking phones for a gun and then shooting African-American boys; blacks have been shot and killed and shot and wounded without the cops ever having seen a gun. Here you have a weapon on full display—not once, but two encounters—and then the guy just walks away. The unspoken reality for us is we know the difference. I'm glad the white guy didn't get shot, but really?

It was the most outrageous thing I've seen in a long time. Total police incompetence. I know, because in my twenty-eight-year career serving the community as a member of the Portland Police Bureau, I used to train cops in defensive tactics. So I understand how this incident should have gone down. And I can tell you we weren't trained to shoot at a target we couldn't see. And you definitely don't allow a suspected gunman to break your containment and escape by simply sauntering off.

When we were finally allowed to go outside, I walked over to my boat to assess the damage: I initially counted twenty-two bullet holes. I saw several officers there who I knew and asked one of the sergeants how this could have happened. He shrugged. Nobody had an answer. Except to say call Risk Management; they pay up to $5,000 for damages like this.

Never in a thousand years did I think my competition ski boat would get shot up by the police in front of my house. And a shooting on a Sunday morning in Laurelhurst, one of the city's most upscale neighborhoods? It was unheard of! And the odd thing is no police report of the officer-involved shooting incident was made public. They're probably thinking, "We can't write this up cuz no matter how we do it, it makes us look like idiots." But they did initiate an Internal Affairs investigation, no doubt because they believe some serious violations occurred. It's classic stonewalling. Build as much time and distance as possible between the incident and when the report is released so people lose interest.

But what pisses me off the most is the response from some people at the bureau who thought it was a big joke my boat got shot up: "Ha-ha, Anderson's done got his comeuppance..." Now, I would be hard pressed to say there was any malice involved, but there's always been a percentage of officers who think my black butt shouldn't be living in a predominantly white neighborhood like this. And once they found out it was my house, then it was all hush-hush—let's do our secret investigation and get out of here. Never a concern about what's happened to my family. You shoot up a police officer's boat in front of his house and the chief should have had his butt down here: "Hey, man, you alright? Your wife? Kids? We're sorry this happened; here's a check to go get you another boat. And have a great summer!" None of that happened. Why? Cuz they're all covering their asses. They're all scared to death, not knowing what Larry Anderson is going to do. My friends on the force said the Risk Management guy was afraid to call me. What are you scared to call me for? Am I going to shoot him? Have I ever whooped anybody's ass ever on the police bureau? Naw, I should have; I should have whooped a whole lot of people's asses. But it's that same thing where white folks think they need to protect themselves from these black men—they're dangerous, they're a menace. And that's what is causing the types of behavior we're seeing playing out across this country. This is why you see black guys getting shot and killed and white guys walking away.

Of course, it was common knowledge I had been very vocal about what was wrong with the police bureau while I was there and when I left. One of the issues I exposed was the reality of racial profiling, and a lot of white officers were upset about that. And then I was very critical of the Special Emergency Response Team because in training they would use pictures of young black men as their shooting targets and make comments they thought were funny—just like shooting up my boat. It's the same sentiment—they don't see the harm they do, the impact they have, they just see it as a big joke. And, hey, we're just doing our job, and what's your problem? Well, my problem is you didn't do your job, and you created a hostile dangerous environment in front of my family. You damaged my boat unnecessarily and now you're gone, and I'm shuffled off to Risk Management. Yeah, I've been critical about certain wrongs I've seen in the Portland Police Bureau. So it wasn't that far-fetched for me to connect the dots in the response I've gotten from them, basically: "Well, Larry, you know, who cares if your boat got shot up? You're lucky we didn't shoot you!"

Well, I'll tell you who cares about that boat. That boat was a personal ministry of mine reaching out to young African-American boys. Been using it for years as a means to create fellowship, take them out on the water, keep them off the streets. I bought the boat, restored it, and a lot of the guys worked with me on fixing it up just right with a tower package for skiing. It was the vehicle I used to spend time with young men who maybe didn't have dads around or a boat to ride in. And it's not just about the damage to the boat, it's about lost time and lost momentum we had with Boys2Men, a mentoring program for young men without fathers. I had promised to take those kids skiing. It's ironic; we had the boat ready for the season. We were supposed to get it on the water that week. Another one of those promises that didn't happen. How do you measure that? The kids were devastated. And the boat is a total loss.

A number of people have suggested I should talk to the mayor, who was also serving as Police Commissioner at the time. Because he's been listening; he's not in denial like other City of Portland mayors have been before. He's made statements already that have acknowledged the city's racist past. Like in his search for a new police chief, the mayor wrote in the job announcement:

> The state of Oregon and its largest city, Portland, share a history of legally sanctioned systemic racism with legally enforced exclusionary practices. Given this history, the successful candidate must demonstrate the capacity and commitment to expand on existing strategies to involve relationships with and service of business to Portland's community of color, ensuring that equity is a bedrock of policing in Portland.

Although that posting raised the ire of the police union, who complained the mayor was calling Portland police officers racist, I received his statement as a step in the right direction. Finally, there was a government official who in his official capacity was giving light and weight and consideration to Portland's systemic racist track record.

What happened to me in the aftermath of my property getting destroyed by the cops is not just an unfortunate isolated incident. This is the result of a lingering atmosphere of oppression and white supremacy that black people have had to deal with for years. There's an undertone that makes me as a black man always have to ask the additional question of, "Did this happen to me because of the color of my skin?" Unlike white people, who don't have to ask that question. Their typical response? Gee, that was unfortunate.

The difference between us is this is reality for me every day; it's just an experiment for white people. Every day I have to live with the possibility of what happened in front of my house. I have to deal with these ignorant white folks who think they should live in Laurelhurst and I shouldn't. No matter how hard I worked and what God has given me, I can't tell them nothing. So psychologically, yeah, I can believe my boat was targeted because in white boys' psyche they don't want me to have stuff like that.

Now, I can have a fishing boat; I don't know how many times white people have asked, "Oh, you going to do some fishing?" *Does this look like a fishing boat to you?!* Here's the perception if I look through their lens: Black guys aren't supposed to have a boat like that cuz professional water skiing is exclusively a white sport. What black person got time to be doing that? Your butt needs to be working, get a job, and take care of your community. Be a good representation and credit to your race. You ain't got no time for leisure and paying the kind of money it takes to have a ski boat. At least when you're out there you need to be doing something productive—like catching fish.

I get no shortage of awkward stares when I'm backing my boat into the water. When I take my friend, Daniel, who is white, people come up to him on the dock and ask about *his* boat. When he points at me and tells them I'm the owner, they just walk away with this perplexed look on their face. This stuff goes on all the time. It's just another example of how the culture affects how we see what we're seeing.

I know what I'm talking about because for the past twenty-five years I've been involved in a so-called racial reconciliation movement here in Portland. Thousands of black, white, and brown men have crossed the threshold of our *Friday* group meetings in our efforts to build friendships across the chasms that have divided us for eons. And this in a city recognized as one of the most racist, most segregated, and least churched in the nation.

So, after more than 1,200 encounters between my white brothers and my black brothers, what great wisdom can I impart about "racial reconciliation?" It's a lie. False advertising. People are trying to create a truth that doesn't exist. Because how can you achieve reconciliation if there's never been conciliation in the beginning? There can only be reconciliation to God, which then eliminates the black/white factor. Because the Bible says there's only one human race. Yes, we bleed the same red blood, but that's not how we've become defined. We're defined by someone's definition of the color and texture of our skin. And then they use that for the benefit of one to the detriment of the other. Black/white is never going to be reconciled because that designation has its origin in hatred, prejudice, and injustice. As long as I see myself as a black man and you see yourself as a white man, by the very nature of our definition we're meant to oppose each other. And God doesn't recognize no black man and no white man. He don't recognize those designations, so therefore if we come to him with that designation we're already in denial of his truth, which means we're unreconciled to him. So when we continue to propagate that in the name of Christian reconciliation, we are in denial of the actual truth of God. And we're placating to what our cultural society has defined our roles to be. Ask a white man what his role in his culture is. How is he viewed? The fact white people haven't thought about that is the definition. I have to think about it all the time because it's constantly before me.

People have defined the message of our *Friday* movement as racial reconciliation, but it never has been; it's never declared itself as that. What we've discovered is that as long as we've got black men and white men talking about "race," there will never be reconciliation. We've got to get men of God talking about first needing to reconcile to our Creator; then you go about figuring out how to love your neighbor.

The problem in our nation today is we're operating in our false identities as white and black people, which has facilitated racism as a major stronghold. Yet we have a country of white folks who don't want to even have the discussion and black folks who get stuck in white folks' definition of us. As a result, there's no real discussion taking place. But we need to wake up! The strongholds of race and racism that separate us into some made-up categories of humanity have no biblical foundation. And once you buy into a lie, God has nothing to do with that. All that has to be eradicated. And that's what makes our *Friday* movement so radical—on our own we can't defeat the evil of racism; we need God's power to stop that mess.

I had no intention of being a minister to white people. In fact, the term "preacher" to me is repulsive. But every time I'm invited to address hundreds of white people at the National Prayer Breakfast in Washington, DC, or as the keynote speaker at the Portland Business Luncheon's Christmas event, I hear the following after speaking God's truth to the white culture: "You're a black guy, how dare you talk to us like that!" Well, I ask back, did you even hear what I had to say? Did you hear the words? "Yeah, but you can't know that!"

Oh man, every day this goes on. And the minute I retreat, God sends them right to my front door at six-thirty on a Sunday morning. He says, "Hey, now they outside your house; what you got to say about that?" When I don't say anything, what happens? People in the bureau and the community call me and say we heard what happened. "What you got to say about that?" When I don't say anything to the media about the big screw-up, the mayor's chief of staff calls me and tells me the mayor wants to meet with me. "What you got to say about that?"

Now, there's lots of people in Portland breaking their necks trying to get in front of the mayor. They'll try anything to get face time with him. I avoid that and the mayor calls me. Wants to come to my house and apologize to me and my family. We'll see about that…

That's just how God is. That's been my whole life. I try to avoid white people and he brings them right to my house.

PART ONE

GROWING UP

CHAPTER ONE

Adopted

It was Old Man Vance who crudely introduced me to the concept of racism. I was seven. The Vances lived up the street and I was always playing with their son, Doug. He was one of my best friends. I remember this one time I was over at his house and we were playing, having fun, just being kids. For some reason we went into the house and this old guy—turns out it was Doug's grandfather—yells, "Hey, what's that nigger doing in the house?"

It was the first time I had ever heard that word and I had no idea what it meant. I guess we were kind of in shock because me and Doug just stopped in the living room when he started yelling at us. Then his grandfather turned toward Doug and demanded, "Is that your nigger friend? What's that nigger doing in this house?" I mean, he just kept on. At first I was oblivious. But then I realized he wasn't calling Doug a nigger—just me!

"Yeah, you're that nigger kid from down the street, aren't ya?"

He was kinda pointing at me and I didn't know what to say. I looked around and I saw Mrs. Vance looking all embarrassed. I remember she said something like, "Grandpa, you've got to stop that!" But I don't think he was listening to her.

I was very confused by the whole ordeal. The only thing I could think of was to go home and ask my mother about it. I remember walking into the kitchen and asking her, "Mom, am I a nigger?"

POW! She slapped me in the face as hard as she could. As I was reeling I remember her saying, "Boy, don't you ever say that word!"

Whooie! I mean, man, that hurt! Now, my mom, she wasn't one to reserve physical discipline, but usually I could associate it with something I had done wrong, like breaking a window or stealing candy. But this? All I could figure out at the time was there's something bad about that word; you don't say that word. I never associated it with me, though, I just thought it was like profanity or cursing. But I was smart enough to know if I ever said that word again in front of my mother I would get another smack. So I never repeated it. And that was the end of it. There was no explanation, never really a discussion with my family as a young child about that word. I just knew, well, that hurt, so don't say that word again.

It was 1963, and my adopted family—the Andersons—had broken a color barrier of sorts by moving into an otherwise all-white neighborhood in Northeast Portland. We weren't rich, by any means, but my dad worked for the railroad and my mom was a Licensed Practical Nurse. They worked hard all their lives and were able to buy the five-bedroom house where we lived. We also had brand new cars and I wore clean clothes, so we were comfortable.

I really wasn't aware as a young child how fortunate I was to have been adopted into the Anderson family. I was a baby child of my birth mother— Carol Jean Washington—who was so poor her mother told her if she had another child she would have to give it up because she couldn't take care of it. She had already raised six children with five different fathers under one small roof. And I later learned that my siblings from our birth mother grew up in poverty. And one of those sisters of mine was killed in prison.

But I don't believe I was given up for adoption because I wasn't loved. In fact, I think my birth mother and her mother wanted the very best for me. But they were poor. And "Big Mama Wilson"—Carol's mom—convinced her it would be impossible to bring up a seventh child in that tiny house. They agreed it would be in everybody's best interest for me to grow up with another family. But not just any family.

Whereas most mothers who put a child up for adoption find an agency first, and then the adoption agency finds a suitable family for the child, Carol and her mom wanted to handpick the mom and dad who would raise me. So while she was still pregnant, Carol—with Big Mama's help—went on a mission to find the perfect mother to raise me, her unborn son. They found their ideal match in Lirlean Anderson, an LPN who spent her career working at nearby Emanuel Hospital. Carol knew of Lirlean because they both worked at the

hospital, but it was Big Mama who lobbied hard for Mrs. Anderson. I learned later Big Mama had lived three houses down from Lirlean and Credrict Anderson before they moved to their house in Northeast Portland, and she had apparently observed the Andersons raise three children. She must have been impressed with their parenting skills because she told Carol she wanted "that nice Christian lady who lived down the street" to take me as her own.

I found out years later my adoption wasn't a slam dunk. Both Lirlean and Credrict

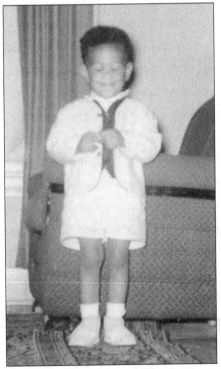

I was adopted at birth and given the name Lawrence Bob Anderson.

Anderson worked full-time, and their oldest daughter didn't necessarily approve. But Dad cast the deciding vote to adopt me because he wanted a son to carry on the Anderson name. I was born Frank Washington, but three weeks later I came home to be with my new family. They named me Lawrence Bob Anderson, which everyone shortened to Larry.

I was adopted into a family with much older siblings—Peggy and Clark were fifteen and twenty years older than I was, and I never really knew them. And while Hilda was quite a bit older, too, she was still around during my formative years. And then there was Phyllis, a little sister my parents took in as a foster child after I was adopted. She became my closest playmate.

I still played with Doug Vance—rode bikes, built forts, terrorized the younger kids—just like the other boys our age. But whenever Doug's ornery grandfather visited, I chose to keep my distance. I was kind of amazed that even after the name-calling incident my mom didn't tell me to be wary of white people (but that did change when I got older). In fact, white people were at our home quite often. Granted, we lived in an all-white neighborhood, but Mom made a point of having neighbors over, regardless the color of their skin. She even volunteered to be a den mother for the local Cub Scout pack, which was made up mostly of white kids. And she was fine with me going to my Cub Scout meetings at white peoples' homes. As far as she was concerned, kids were kids, and she chose not to contaminate my innocence by pointing out racial disparities. Sadly, I learned all too soon from the other kids just how wide the gap was between my black friends and my white friends.

One late-summer evening Doug and I went on a secret mission. Well, that's what we called it, but it was really a race to or from some grave danger that took us two good guys through the alleys and backyards of our neighbors' homes. We must have misread our coordinates because, after about a half hour of scaling walls and jumping fences, we found ourselves in enemy territory—west of Fifteenth Street. West of Fifteenth Street was where my

birth family lived. It was the area with the highest concentration of
families. It wasn't necessarily "the other side of the tracks," but even at a
early age I recognized I enjoyed a certain kind of privileged lifestyle my other
family didn't have.

The kids like me who lived on the east side of that boundary knew if you
wanted to find trouble, just cross that road. West of Fifteenth was where the
Mayo boys lived. Wayne and his brothers apparently didn't appreciate me
and my white friend running around in "their" backyards.

So they chased us. And when they caught us, one of the Mayo brothers
pulled me aside and demanded to know what I was doing hanging out
with a white boy. While one of them held me back, the others proceeded
to beat the crap out of Doug. I got pushed around a bit when I tried to help
Doug, but they didn't attack me. So Doug comes home all messed up, and
I'm feeling bad because we were both together and they beat him up and
didn't do anything to me. That was the beginning of my understanding—it's
because he was white.

Years later, while performing my duties as a Portland Police Officer,
I had the distinct pleasure of arresting a couple of those Mayo boys. The
delinquents probably didn't even remember the day—some fifteen years
earlier—when they had pummeled that little white kid named Doug Vance.
But I never forgot. Those two childhood memories—Old Man Vance calling
me the derogatory slur I was never supposed to repeat, and the Mayos tar-
geting my white friend, but not me—instilled in my young mind there was
definitely a difference between "us and them." Before, I had been oblivious
to the ugly concept of racism, but sadly, even before I started kindergarten, I
was gaining a measure of awareness that because people had different skin
colors they treated each other differently.

CHAPTER TWO

Privileged

The only black person I ever saw growing up was a maid at my grand-parents' house. We lived on the west side of Portland and, as far as I can remember, I never saw a child of other ethnicity the entire time we lived in Oregon. That would have been from the year I was born in 1946 to the late 1950s when we moved away. Southwest Portland was absolutely all white. All my playmates were white. All the kids at Maplewood Elementary were white, just like Elizabeth Hayhurst, where I got trans-ferred to in the fourth grade. There were certainly no black children in my Sunday school classes at Portland Foursquare Church where my parents and grandparents were longtime members. And it didn't get much whiter than being part of a family business that raised cows to produce milk, which white men in white uniforms delivered to area homes in white trucks.

But that didn't mean me, my older brother, Rod, and cousin, Carl, were oblivious to the fact that black people lived in Portland, Oregon. That's because we interacted almost daily with a black woman. Her name was Irene. And she was the housemaid for my grandparents, Henry and Rosina Cadonau, who owned Alpenrose Dairy.

Irene was the sweetest woman you'd ever want to meet, a true woman of God. She took the bus to and from her home in the north part of the city, but sometimes when she worked late Grandpa Henry would drive her home and I would ride along. It was during those trips to the other side of town I began to recognize what made people different: where they lived, what they wore, even the way they talked. It's kind of sad, but my knowledge of Irene was sort of an indoctrination into how white people in the fifties interacted with blacks—as servants. Right out of the movie *The Help*.

I still have this painful memory as a little boy when I called my cousin "nigger" in front of Irene. I really didn't even know what the word meant—I had probably heard it somewhere and repeated it—but from the hurt and disgusted look on Irene's face, I knew it was wrong. I saw a pain on that sweet woman's face that I was responsible for, and I didn't ever want to see it again. I have no memory of ever saying that word again.

Even though I wasn't aware of it as a child, as I matured I began to realize just how well off our family was. Spending your childhood at Alpenrose was like going to Disneyland every day. Over the years, my grandparents had transformed their fifty-two acres of rolling hills into a destination for family fun and sporting events. The dairy was much more than a pen for cows, a milking parlor, and a bottling plant. They built an authentic-looking Old West town, complete with a general store, post office, livery stable, hotel, ice cream parlor, Western Union office, and an opera house for community concerts and events. I'm pretty sure every kid who grew up in Southwest Portland since the fifties has been to Alpenrose on a school field trip to visit the Old West town, ride a pony, eat ice cream, and maybe milk a cow.

Having grandparents who owned a successful business like that was obviously a privilege, but I didn't realize at the time I was a privileged kid. I just knew I had access to a lot of stuff other people didn't have—like riding one of my grandfather's fifty ponies around Southwest Portland.

I think it was my third-grade buddy, Tim Tyler, who informed me my grandparents were rich. One day after school we walked up the hill to the dairy from my house down the street and I showed him around. He kept saying "That's amazing!" as I pointed out things in the house my grandparents had collected from their travels. Like the display of fifteen or so big brass Swiss cowbells, which they would put on the cows for special occasions. In the main great room in front of the fireplace was a big black bearskin turned into a rug. Grandpa had shot it in Alaska or Canada on a hunting trip. Tim was absolutely fascinated with it. The head had been turned into a big growling face, with the tongue and inside of the mouth made of something like pink plaster, but I think the teeth were real. The fur was soft and we lay down on it and wiggled around on it like two spoiled kids.

Riding one of grandpa's ponies at Alpenrose was a favorite summer pastime.

Irene made an impression on Tim, too. One, for being the first black person he had ever met, and, second, he told me he still has this vivid memory of her shooing us out of the house because we were raiding the pantry. We got caught in the act of gobbling up some of the maraschino cherries and green olives Grandpa kept on hand for parties. We had a good laugh about it, but what a sticky mess we made!

It really was an idyllic lifestyle for me and my brother growing up at Alpenrose, especially in the summer with three months off from school to play outdoors in the warm Oregon sunshine. We would roam the hills on a couple of grandpa's ponies, shooting our .22 rifles, playing war games, and generally harassing the cows and the milkers. One summer after we had torn up our grandparents' backyard playing baseball with some friends, Grandpa had an area in front of the barn bulldozed to create a dirt ball field. When he saw us kids chasing errant baseballs all over the place, he built a backstop, and then an outfield fence. The Alpenrose baseball diamond became so popular and well-used he built two more, and the facility became the preferred site for area Little League games. And when I got into quarter midget racing as a ten- and eleven-year-old, Grandpa built a dirt race track.

Life was good at the dairy. Both my parents, Anita and Ray, worked there, with Anita's mom and dad in charge of the family operation. Dairy life is a seven-days-a-week commitment, but the Cadonaus and the Birklands (except my dad) set Sundays aside for church. I would say I was raised in a very religious family because it seemed to me we went to every church service they had at Portland Foursquare. I mean, we went early morning to Sunday school where my mom taught, with church next at eleven. Then there was an evening five o'clock cadet service, and after that an evening church service. So church was all day; it was continual Pentecostal instruction.

My grandmother was the spiritual champion of the family, a devout Christian woman who knew the Bible inside and out. I mean, anytime anything came up she had a scripture to quote. In a way it drove me nuts, but in another way I realized the Word was just part of her life. But the thing I remember most is Grandma praying. Whenever I stayed overnight, she would put me to bed and then pause to pray over me for a while. Sometimes longer. I remember this one time, I was lying in bed and Grandma came over and started to pray. It went on for quite a bit and I must have fallen asleep—I don't know how long I was asleep, could have been five minutes, could have been half an hour. But when I came back to my senses a little while later she was still praying! For her it wasn't some perfunctory ritual to put me to bed: "Now I lay me down to sleep…okay we're done." She was actually praying for me. She was actually believing for me. I was just a little boy at the time, but that had a real impact on me. She wasn't just praying because she thought it was a good thing to do, she was praying because she actually believed God would answer her prayers.

I know one of Grandma's fervent prayers was that I would receive Jesus Christ as my Lord and Savior. As a little kid, I do remember one Sunday morning going forward when they gave the altar call and praying with Mrs. Matson, one of my parent's friends, to receive Jesus. It seemed real to me at the time. But it was a church summer camp experience that really solidified my faith. I was twelve years old and, just like the previous couple of summers, my parents sent me to Camp Crestview, a Foursquare retreat center. We would spend a good portion of the week hiking the trails overlooking the majestic Columbia River, but the focus was on the Bible and learning how to become followers of Jesus. At previous church camps, I remember joining the others in praying the "sinner's prayer," but my words may have been an emotional response that seemed heartfelt at the time.

Everybody got saved at camp. Sometimes you'd hold out until Thursday, sometimes you'd get saved early, but you'd get saved every summer when you went there. But this one particular summer when I was twelve, something happened in my heart. I mean, I really believed in Jesus. He was very real to me. It was transformative. In fact, my religious experience was so impactful I determined to share the good news with others. I planned it all out, figuring the ideal opportunity to go public with my faith decision would be the first day of school when everyone was asked the obligatory question, "What did you do this summer?" So, when it was my turn, I bravely walked to the front of my seventh-grade class and announced what I had done that summer: *we went to Disneyland.*

I had literally plotted this out. I was going to give my personal testimony. I was going to declare I believed in Jesus. Well, I chickened out. I mean, I did. It was a missed opportunity, but for me it felt like more of a denial. Immediately after I made that lame comment about going to the Magic Kingdom, I could see in my mind's eye the Bible verse from Matthew: "Whosoever therefore shall confess me before men, him will I confess also before my Father which is in heaven. But whosoever shall deny me before men, him will I also deny before my Father which is in heaven."

I felt profoundly guilty. And ashamed. But instead of clinging fast to my faith and drawing closer to God, I just kind of drifted away from him. It's like at that moment I felt defeated. I felt like I had denied Jesus. I felt as if I had failed. And that was a pivotal point in my life because that disappointment initiated the start of a downhill slide.

I wasn't even a teenager yet and I was already experiencing a crisis of faith. I knew I believed in Jesus. And something real had happened that day at church camp. So why, when given a chance to acknowledge my relationship with Jesus, did I choose not to? It was a confusing time. Just a few weeks earlier I had experienced a spiritual high; now I was freefalling into a period of darkness, a phase of my life that led to illicit ways and a brush with the law.

Sure, I was a good kid from an affluent family, and when I stole stuff it was usually just candy or clothes I shoplifted. But then, for no good reason, I stole a gun...just to shoot it. There were other violations, but most of them misdemeanors and most of them unprosecuted at the time. I was a rebellious twelve-year-old, but things were about to get worse. By the time I turned thirteen the summer of 1959, the Birkland family would be busted up and the privileged life I had enjoyed at Alpenrose would be disrupted forever.

CHAPTER THREE

Bullied

My mom was very aware of the challenges I would face growing up as one of the only African-American kids in a white neighborhood. That's because she had spent most of a thirty-year career working at a white institution that treated her unfairly. She was an LPN, but she had the equivalent education of a Registered Nurse. The problem was at the time they wouldn't promote black women to RN status. Just LPN, which meant she could give shots and change bedpans.

When I was young she was something like a visiting nurse and she used to drag me along to all these very nice homes up in the West Hills. She would give them pills, take blood samples, and clean out bedpans—to me it just seemed like maid work. Later on that would affect me because it proved education for black people don't mean nothin'. You can be educated and qualified, but ain't nobody going to respect that. Back then I couldn't articulate that, but it left a big imprint on me as I got older. The other memory I still can't shake is standing in line with my mother at Woolworth's…and watching her be ignored! My mother had the grace to stand there while white people behind us got served first. To this day, having someone cut in front of me pisses me off more than anything.

was aware of the odds—it was no secret the economic
ions in our county heavily favored the dominant white
l to white families, blacks earned about half the annual
...a nad double the unemployment rate. But the two statistics most troubling to her were the lower-than-fifty-percent high school graduation rate for African Americans and the much higher likelihood black youths would be charged with a crime.

She used to harp on me there was nothing she and my dad wanted more than for me to get an education. And to graduate high school. So she did her best to keep me out of trouble by making sure I was busy with Cub Scouts, church, and sports. Plus, she was always lecturing me to do the right thing, to make good choices and not just go along with the crowd. And if I strayed she didn't have a problem administering a whooping.

She didn't have any issue either with other parents getting on me whenever I got out of line. It was like I had this extended family committed to keeping me on the straight and narrow. It was kind of bizarre to me because it seemed every adult knew each other. And they knew everybody's kids. They knew your mother's name. They knew your father's name. They knew where they worked. And they all had the green light to dole out punishment. Us kids knew it as "permission," which meant all the other parents had the blessing from our moms and dads to beat your butt. Basically, any adult could discipline any child at any time for anything. I just figured all the adults in the world must be in cahoots with each other because I couldn't get away with any mischief.

There was this one brief moment in my childhood when I thought I had outsmarted the grownups. It was during the time my mom was an usher at our church. Allen Temple was a few blocks from our house and some Sundays when she would have to go early I would walk there on my own. Mom would leave me money for the offering, but the coins never made it into the basket. That's because I would stop at Sam & Ollie's Market on the way. I should have known from past experience Ms. Ollie would tell my mom I was buying candy instead of tithing. I felt pretty sure I was getting away with it because my mom never told me she got those calls from Ms. Ollie. But one Sunday my grace period expired. My foolish pride got the best of me and I decided to steal the candy and keep the money. Of course, Ms. Ollie caught me in the act. And then she grabbed the phone to call my mom. Knowing how much trouble I would be in, I begged her not to tell. I promised I would work off the damages—just so long as my mother never found out about the theft. For the next several weeks I paid off my debt to Ms. Ollie by taking out the garbage and sweeping floors. I'll never forget that lesson—stealing stuff ain't worth it.

That was the type of community I grew up in, where it was kinda good and kinda bad everyone knew your business. But while the vast majority of people in our neighborhood were Caucasian, I began to drift away from my white friends like Doug Vance. Our church was an all-black congregation and that's where I developed a lot of friendships. My parents were big on family gatherings and so I was always around my uncles, always hanging out with my cousins. We would have at least twenty people over for holidays and special events—it wasn't until I got older I realized half those people weren't really related to us.

Being around other blacks gave me a sense of who I was, a sense of purpose. Around them I never felt out of place. I just felt drawn in to the comfort and security of my tight-knit black community. And in the process, I became much more aware of the distinction between how white kids were treated and how black kids were looked at and treated.

It was during this phase of my upbringing where stories were shared about the mistreatment of blacks at the hands of white people. We were told white people have no soul. That they can't be trusted. That they're devoid of the rhythm of life. I was only eight or nine and—even though I couldn't explain it—I knew there was something that wasn't good between black folks and white folks.

But one thing I couldn't reconcile in my young mind was if things were so bad between white and black, how come our all-black congregation bowed down to this picture of some white Norwegian-looking dude on the wall that somebody told me is Jesus? I'm seeing the civil rights marches on TV and I'm looking at white policemen beating up black folks and turning dogs loose on them. And I'm supposed to be some good Christian and worship this white guy from the painting on the wall? No, I decided right then if that's what Christianity is about, I ain't going to have anything to do with it. It took *years* for me to get that thought and that image of religion out of the way so I could see God as he is.

As a young boy experiencing all this, I learned from white people how to hate. Now I didn't learn this from my mother, who had grace and never hated

white people. So I hated them for her; I felt it was my responsibility. I just did all the hating quietly, because my mother didn't play that. But in my heart I developed the wrong attitude. Oh, on the outside I knew how to have great appearances, because white people were a necessary evil and I couldn't just banish them from my life. And even though I was all messed up inside, I learned how to play the game. I learned how to pretend; my "faith" became a lie and a pretense.

Growing up in an all-white neighborhood wasn't a problem...until the bullying began.

I don't know if it was due to this awakening I was experiencing at that point in my life, but conflicts with white kids became more prevalent—and personal—at Sabin School where I attended through eighth grade. First it was a white kid named David Welby with whom I was at war. David, who was two years older and a couple inches taller than me, would take my bike, push me to the ground, and call me names. I vowed to get even someday when I was bigger, but for a long time the bullying continued.

I was a pretty easy target because I was a skinny kid who walked like a duck. I was born with both feet almost twisted backwards, so I had to wear special training shoes. They called me "Crazy Legs Anderson" because I walked with my feet pointing outwards, and when I ran my legs didn't go straight back and forth, but all over the place. So people said it looked like I had crazy legs.

But crooked feet or not, my funny gait didn't inhibit my athletic prowess. Beginning in fourth grade and continuing through eighth, me and my fellow Sabin Bombers dominated all comers—winning city championships five years in a row in basketball, flag football, *and* softball. But I just didn't look all that athletic, so I was constantly challenged by older kids at school.

One day this black kid named Donnie Carter, who was two grades ahead of me, confronted me on the basketball court and challenged me to a game of one-on-one. He upped the ante by calling me a punk who couldn't even walk normal. I kicked his butt. And after I beat him I threw down some in-your-face smack talk, which only made him angrier. Donnie retaliated by punching me in the face and taking away my basketball. I was able to wrestle it back and I took off, crazy legs and all, running for home—with Donnie giving chase.

That after-school scene became a daily occurrence for the next couple of weeks. As soon as the final bell rang, students rushed outside to watch Donnie Carter try to catch Crazy Legs Larry Anderson as I ran the three blocks up the hill to my house. Then one day I got tired of the taunts I was a

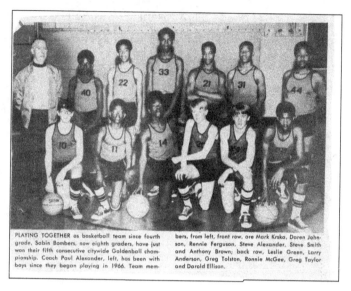

PLAYING TOGETHER as basketball team since fourth grade, Sabin Bombers, now eighth graders, have just won their fifth consecutive citywide Goldenball championship. Coach Paul Alexander, left, has been with boys since they began playing in 1966. Team members, from left, front row, are Mark Krska, Daren Johnson, Rennie Ferguson, Steve Alexander, Steve Smith and Anthony Brown; back row, Leslie Green, Larry Anderson, Greg Tolston, Ronnie McGee, Greg Taylor and Darold Ellison.

My Sabin Bombers team also won multiple city-wide championships in flag football and softball.

coward. That day I decided to wait for Donnie on the basketball court, and with a crowd gathering to witness the fight, I let the bully know I was done running. I really don't know what came over me, but something changed inside me that day. I just jumped all over him. I was scared, mad, insane—all of that. I jumped on him and I whooped his ass good.

That was an important turning point in my young life. It came with the realization Donnie Carter was the one who was scared now. He was the punk, not me. And the other older kids who had been picking on me? I figured if they were confronted by someone who wasn't afraid, who wouldn't back down, they were probably just as scared as Donnie was. I knew if I just stood my ground I wouldn't be called a coward anymore. And I wouldn't have to run from people anymore. That's when all the fighting started.

With my newfound confidence, I didn't necessarily seek out opportunities to fight, but I didn't hesitate to protect myself or someone I felt was being picked on unfairly. I hated it when bigger kids took advantage of those who couldn't defend themselves. And if two guys jumped somebody, I would be right in the middle of it, trying to protect the one. I especially couldn't stand it when white boys would rough up a black kid. So I became the avenger in our neighborhood. I would go after the bullies, the guys who took advantage of people who couldn't protect themselves.

Of course, in some people's eyes, that made me the bully because I bullied the bulliers. But I didn't have an issue with that. In my mind I had drawn a line in the sand—I vowed never to beat up on or bully those who couldn't protect themselves. While I didn't win every fight, I earned the reputation of someone who wouldn't back down when challenged.

Fortunately for me and my black schoolmates (who made up about fifteen percent of the Sabin school population), there was another outlet for aggressive behavior—sports. We could get in trouble for fighting in school, but on the ball field we could take out our frustrations on any well-deserving candidate. Some of those recipients included certain white boys me and my friend, Greg Taylor, would tackle extra hard. Fighting could get us kicked off the team, but hard hits on the field were applauded. As we grew bigger and stronger, we took a certain amount of joy avenging ourselves on the field of competition for perceived injustices.

Other than sports, school didn't interest me much. Whether it was basketball, football, baseball, or track, I learned how to compete at a high level and earned a reputation as one of the better athletes in town. The classroom? It was only a means to an end. And the best thing about playing sports year-round was it kept me out of trouble. Sure, me and the boys would sneak out at night, run the streets and maybe break some windows, vandalize a couple of cars, or raid the neighbors' fruit trees. But the truth was we didn't want to get into any kind of real trouble that would get us kicked off the team.

Fortunately for me (and my career in sports), I spent most of my summers in Center Point, Texas, where my mom was from. It was cool because we got to ride the train for free because of Dad's job. The other benefit was those annual trips effectively limited my hangout time on the streets of Portland. I figure if it wasn't for sports and those busy summers, I would probably be dead or in jail.

As a youngster, I was kind of rebellious and acted out a bit, but my behavior never got to the point where I had any interaction with the law enforcement community. There was no need because my parents were very involved in my life. They were the police. I feared my mom's wrath much more than I did any man in a police uniform. But it wasn't for lack of opportunities to stray to the wrong side of the law.

I did have a close call with the cops one day when me and my two buddies were hanging out at the mall and they decided to steal a woman's purse. I begged off, telling Andrew and Melvin if they did something that low they wouldn't be my friends anymore. So, after I stopped at the candy store to buy some caramel corn, I left the Lloyd Center. But as I exited the lower level, I noticed two women at the pay phone, one of whom was pointing at me. I figured they must be the victims of my former friends' antics. When the police nabbed me a few blocks away, I explained it was a matter of mistaken identity. But the cops weren't hearing any of that. They tried to grab me and force me into their patrol car, but I started wrestling with them—and one of them slipped and fell. I was being totally defiant because my feeling was you don't grab people and bully them, especially when they're innocent. Eventually, the three of us were tussling and wrestling on the ground and I told them I would stop if they wouldn't handcuff me. When we stood back up, they told me the guys had pushed the lady to the ground in the process of snatching her purse. That made me so angry I not only identified them but offered to take the officers to Andrew's home—where they arrested him. And then to Melvin's home—where they arrested him, too. I guess I could have been arrested, too, for assaulting a police officer, but when they figured out my loyalty was on the right side of the law they let me go. That experience—including the officer's explanation to my mother that exoner-ated me—softened something inside me about how I viewed the police.

I then told all my friends if they ever did stupid stuff like that, we ain't friends no more, we ain't cool. I will be the first person to tell on your ass. I will turn you in and hope you go to jail where you belong.

I give my parents a lot of credit for instilling in me a core set of values that have stuck with me my entire life. Plus, I knew my mom would kill me if I ever got brought home in a police car. That only happened once, and although I'm still alive to talk about it, I couldn't sit down for days afterward.

CHAPTER FOUR

The Pancake House

Was it a sin to not profess I had given my life to the Lord? Maybe not, but I had committed in my heart to tell my seventh-grade classmates about my Camp Crestview religious experience. And then I reneged on that promise. Here I was, this church-going kid who had confessed Jesus as my Lord and Savior at summer camp, who was all excited about sharing his testimony...and then I pulled a Peter—the disciple who denied knowing Jesus three times the night before he was crucified. And instead of getting back on the right path to redemption, I wandered away from my Christian roots.

I began to rebel against authority. Stole stuff. Got into trouble. And what I probably needed more than anything else—the stability and support of my extended family at Alpenrose—was crumbling. Dad had an affair. With one of the quarter midget racing moms.

As a wholesale sales rep for the dairy, Dad was gone a lot and I was sort of used to him being out of town. But one day he didn't come home at all. My mom sat me and my brother down and told us he had moved to California. While we didn't fully understand the circumstances of the breakup, it was pretty clear to me and Rod you can't be in good standing with a boss who happens to be your father-in-law if you're having an affair while married to his daughter. Turns out his cheating on her wasn't the only thing wrong with their marriage. He was mean to Mom, just downright horribly abusive to her. And I hated him for that.

I didn't know just how unhappy my mother was in the relationship until years after they died and I discovered a letter she had written in 1942. In part, it read:

> We've been married three-and-a-half years, with many long months and longer days. It's been a continual turmoil, relieved here and there by only brief intervals of fatigue. We fought but never won. Marriage to him has been nothing more than an unfortunate blunder.

I cried when I read that letter. Pathetic. Awful. Those were the words that came to mind.

A lot of people were counseling mom to divorce dad, but she wouldn't. In fact, there was talk of a reconciliation about a year after my parents separated. The relationship with the other woman had ended and dad had started a new chapter in his life in Southern California. With $5,000 borrowed from his life insurance policy, he had negotiated the rights to open an Original Pancake House restaurant franchise in Anaheim. The "original" Original Pancake House was located just a few miles from Alpenrose Dairy, so I'm guessing he had gotten to know the owners and their operation pretty well.

I really had no idea what my dad was up to, so when he invited me to visit him in Anaheim over spring break "to see what it would be like to live in California," I decided to go. Of course, I liked the sunny spring weather in Southern California (compared to the cold and wet of Oregon's springtime) and thought the restaurant was kind of cool. It was on the ground floor of a large renovated house with living quarters upstairs. Five months after my visit, me, my brother, and my mom left our comfortable life at Alpenrose and moved south to live with dad above the Anaheim Original Pancake House. With much trepidation because we had no idea what to expect.

Even though our family was reunited, I was pretty mad at my dad for a long time. They had so-called reconciled, but he was still mean to mom. I remember telling her she should divorce him, but she never did. I would get so upset by the abuse; I remember crying and pounding my fist in the pillow one night, saying to myself, "that so-and-so is never going to make me cry again."

Leaving the comfort and security of Alpenrose to live above a Pancake House was traumatic enough, but I didn't know anybody in Anaheim; I felt like a fish out of water. Ever since I was a kid, I had known everybody at school, church, and the dairy. But when I started

Because of my slicked-back hair, my friends at school called me Elvis.

eighth grade at John C. Fremont Junior High School, I knew no one. I had no friends.

And the friends I eventually did make made fun of me. There was Neal Cooper, who remains a friend even now, who used to call me "Elvis" because I had my hair slicked back. Plus, I was sort of a klutz. One day I showed up at school with two full casts on my arms; I had broken both of them falling off my skateboard. Well, if you can call it that—back then we made our own out of a pair of old roller skates. I had to go to school with casts holding my arms at nine-ty-degree angles. I couldn't eat my lunch without dropping half of it on the floor. Everybody laughed at me. They thought it was hilarious. But it wasn't funny to me.

When my arms finally healed I put them to good use working as a fry cook at the restaurant. Made a buck an hour scrambling eggs, frying bacon, and flipping more than twenty different kinds of pancakes. I did that almost every weekend through junior high and high school, which meant I had a little more spending money than most of my friends.

I remember Neal used to meet me at the Pancake House after my shift was over and we would go hang out together. One time when we were messing around in the living area upstairs, my dad walked down the hall and said something mean to Neal like, "What the hell are you doing up here?" I told him he was my friend and he was just visiting. But Dad just grumbled something and stormed off. Nobody wanted to be around the house when my dad was there. My mother, on the other hand, was loved by everybody. It made me sad when Neal told me my parents seemed completely different, "not like a couple, not like a mom-and-dad couple."

The tension upstairs at the Original Pancake House was one of the reasons I was so anxious to get my driver's license. I was out of the house as soon as I turned sixteen. And like most of my buddies, I headed straight to the beach to pursue my new passion—surfing. It became my escape from all the screaming and yelling at the Pancake House. It was my getaway from school, where my grades were okay but I was no good at sports. But give me an eight-foot board and a six-foot wave and I excelled.

With the money I had saved from making all those silver dollar pancakes, I was able to buy my independence in the form of a red-and-white 1957 Chevy Nomad, tricked out with chrome wheels and chrome trim. The two-door station wagon was ideal for hauling a buddy and two surf boards. At every chance, me and my core group of friends—Neal Cooper, Kim Dedic, and Dick Williams—would pile into our cars and head thirty miles south to our favorite surfing spots near Dana Point. We would drive right past the smaller-wave beaches like Huntington, Newport, and Laguna for the more challenging rides at Doheny and Lower Trestles.

We surfed five days a week, six days if we could, sometimes seven days a week, depending on the weather and the waves. Our last class got out at two-ten and we would be surfing by three. Same thing on the weekend—I worked Saturdays and Sundays until two and then surfed until it got dark.

THE Original ®
PANCAKE HOUSE

1418 E. LINCOLN, ANAHEIM, CA
(714) 535-9915

I earned money flipping pancakes all the way through high school.
[Permission from the Original Pancake House was given to use this photo.]

And I got pretty good at it, too, even though my surfer buddy, Neal, still thought I was a klutz because I was a "goofy-footer," which meant I surfed with my right foot forward, while most everyone else was left foot forward. And I did have one claim to fame. Every weekend the local TV station would feature the top surfers demonstrating their best moves. One time as they were filming a well-known guy riding a wave, I somehow popped up next. Kind of a fluke, but that night on the news they featured me, goofy-foot and all. But because they didn't know who I was, they ran the clip with the voiceover, "An unknown surfer catches a good left at Trestles."

To me, Lower Trestles was the best surfing spot in all of Southern California. Sure, you could catch a decent ride at Upper Trestles, In-Betweens, Church, and Cotton's Point, but due to the slope of the rocky bottom at Lower Trestles, the waves were consistent and the rides were long. I also got a kick out of outsmarting the guardians of that coveted beach area. You could access Trestles by foot—a twenty-to-thirty-minute trek through a jungle of brush—or you could drive through a gate on a government-owned road and park right on the beach. The problem was the gateway to one of the best surfing spots in the state was part of Marine Corps Base Camp Pendleton. So we had to sneak in.

It was like a battle—us against the Marines. They used to love to do surfer duty because for them it was like war without any consequences. Sometimes when we were sneaking in, they were lying in wait and would chase us away. Or if they saw our car parked down there they would do something weird, like steal the valve cores from the tires and deflate them. So I started bringing extra valve cores and a tire pump.

This game between the military and us surfers (okay, us trespassers) eventually got more serious. The Marines figured out which gate we were able to jimmy open and they secured it with a bigger lock. But even that didn't deter us intrepid—albeit naïve—surfer dudes. I thought it was just wrong they wouldn't let us drive down that road. So one time I brought a chisel and was using it to break the lock. Right then a California Highway Patrolman drove up behind us. I was so freaked out I threw the chisel up in the air and it landed at my feet. He took down all my information and let us go, so I thought that was the end of it.

But that wasn't the end of it. A few days later at school I was summoned to the principal's office. I introduced myself to the man in the suit who was waiting for me, thinking he was a new school counselor or administrator.

"I know who you are," said the suit. "I'm with the FBI."

The fed explained I was under investigation for destruction of government property, a Class C felony. He told me people could go to prison for that. When I started babbling excuses about why I thought it was okay for us to surf at the best spot in the entire state, that me and my friends had been driving in there forever, the FBI man interrupted me.

"Well, didn't you think the locked gate with the 'Keep Out' sign meant something?" he asked, with more than a bit of sarcasm.

Knowing I couldn't win that argument, I profusely apologized. He pretty much scared me straight, told me never to do it again. And I didn't. We just walked in from then on.

It was the early sixties, and me and my friends all felt the same way—you had to surf, you just had to do it. Looking back, I realize it was a self-indulgent lifestyle all about fun: a hedonistic culture that revolved around cars, girls, music, dancing, and drinking. The Beach Boys epitomized the era with songs like "Surfin' USA," "California Girls," "Surfer Girl," "Dance, Dance, Dance," and "Fun, Fun, Fun." And movies like *The Endless Summer* and *Big Wednesday* glorified the lure of big waves, girls in bikinis, bonfires on the beach, and partying.

Sometimes my friend Ernie and I surfed five days a week, even six and seven.

For me and my crew, following a week of every-day surfing, a tame weekend might kick off with a Friday night visit to nearby Disneyland. But for some real fun on Saturday nights, me and the guys headed to the Rendezvous Ballroom in Newport Beach to listen to music and dance to our favorite surfer bands—the Righteous Brothers and Dick Dale & His Del-Tones. Of course, we would first get boozed up on beer, vodka, or some cheap wine.

There was no dope smoking or drug use in our group while we were in high school, but we did like our alcohol. Of course, we were too young to buy it, so we had to get creative. But creativity sometimes led to stupidity.

It's not like we were *robbing* liquor stores, but I was definitely shop-lifting from liquor stores. Hey, it's Saturday. And you're going to the dance. But you got no booze! So this one afternoon I drove with my friend, Kim Dedic, to acquire some Southern Comfort whiskey. While Kim stayed in the car, I went in and came running out with a pint. But when we two amateurs realized a pint wasn't going to be enough, I went back in and grabbed another one. This time I got busted. The cops showed up and took me to the police station.

While I dreaded what the police might do to me, it was the unforgettable phone call to my mom that hurt the most:

"Uh, Mrs. Birkland, we've got your son down here at the Anaheim police station," I overheard the lieutenant say. "Yes, well, he stole some whiskey out of Al's Party Pantry. No, no, Mrs. Birkland, there's no mistake...No, Mrs. Birkland, he's admitted to us he drinks whiskey. So, Mrs. Birkland, would you and your husband please come down here and pick him up."

My mom and dad did make that embarrassing trip to the police station, and, as they did in those days, the cops released me into my parents' custody. Although I was a miscreant son, I was fortunate I didn't earn a

41

juvenile record for the theft. But I didn't escape punishment. It was bad enough on the drive home being bombarded with lectures and questions like, "Where have we gone wrong?" and, "How have we failed you?"

I'm thinking, they didn't fail me, I failed myself. I should have stuck with the one pint, you know, and I would have been fine. If I wouldn't have gone back for that second pint, I wouldn't have gotten caught. Now that was stupid!

That incident was the one time I didn't argue with my parents about my punishment. They took my car keys away and wouldn't let me drive for six weeks. That meant walking the mile-and-a-half to and from school. No driving to the Rendezvous Ballroom. And no driving to the beach. Ouch!

Well, I was a thief. You can't argue being a thief. I mean, it's a commandment. You can't argue this is okay. I would argue about what time you're supposed to be home. I'd argue whether smoking was right or wrong, you know. But stealing booze out of Al's Party Pantry, that's a bust. That's theft. I didn't argue. It sucked. And you would've thought I would've changed my ways. Well, I don't recall stealing whiskey after that. At least I don't think I did. We just figured out other ways to get liquor.

You would think I learned my lesson, but my "sticky-finger" habit wasn't limited to swiping bottles of booze. I also liked "shopping" at Norm Meager's, the best men's clothing store in Anaheim. I was very particular about clothes, and I had a certain fondness for Corbin slacks, Indian Madras shirts, and British walkers. I just didn't like paying for them. I preferred the "BOGO" special—buy one, get one free; although the free one was usually tucked under my jacket as I paid for the other pair of pants.

Overall, our antics during junior high and high school were pretty tame—beer, wine, and maybe some vodka or whiskey here and there. That was the extent of our imbibing. Nobody got arrested, nobody did drugs, and even the thought of smoking marijuana was so far beyond belief because we thought weed was for dope addicts. Sure, there was some nefarious behavior amongst our group, some inappropriate activities, but I don't pin that solely on one person. I guess I kind of just went along with the crowd, something I chalked up to my "California experience." I was only sixteen years old, but it was a pivotal time in my life, too, because I could not shake the fact that four years earlier I had denied Jesus. I still believed. Even went sporadically to church with my mom. And I had an awareness I could still opt for a path of righteous living.

But that's not what happened. I began to do more and more of what everybody else did—I just kind of drifted down the road that led to drinking more, shoplifting more, and eventually I got into drugs. Even a miracle couldn't dissuade me from my delinquency.

I was feeling pain in my left ear, so my mom took me in for an X-ray. When the doctor came back into the room, he showed us an image of a tumor and recommended it be surgically removed. But my Grandma Cadonau from Alpenrose offered another option—prayer. She believed in God's ability to heal. So when she arranged for a pastor to pray over my ear, I did not protest.

I vividly remember thinking I've got nothing to lose. Hey, he prays for me, it doesn't work, I get the operation. If he prays for me and it works, I'm off the hook! Well, I didn't feel any different after the pastor prayed for my healing, but at my next doctor's appointment I asked for another X-ray "to see if the tumor was still there." I kind of got my nerve up and told the doctor my pastor had prayed for my healing. He treated me like I was this stupid little kid, which, in a way, I was.

But the doubting doctor did take another X-ray. And when he came back with the X-ray from before and the X-ray after in his hands, he had an incredulous look on his face. He told me and mom it appeared as if the tumor had been surgically removed. But there was no external scar. The tumor was just gone.

Now, as a teenager, I thought that was good news because then I could go surfing, and I didn't have to have the surgery over Christmas vacation. I would like to say I then lived a holy and godly life. But that didn't happen.

CHAPTER FIVE

Basketball or Bust

It was the summer after eighth grade, and I had a little business venture on the side—stealing eight-track tape decks out of cars, fixing them up, and selling them. But my entrepreneurial endeavor was short-lived, interrupted by a cop who witnessed me scoping out some parked cars. When he asked what I was planning to do with the screwdriver and pair of pliers I had in my back pocket, I conjured up some fabrication about needing tools to work on my bicycle. The officer was not convinced I was a bicycle repairman and he promptly invited me to sit in the back seat of his squad car.

When I told him where I lived, he recognized me as Mrs. Anderson's son and proceeded to drive the few blocks to our house. I thought my life was over when he parked in our driveway and told me to stay in the car while he went inside. I'm in the back of a cop car all by myself—bawling, freaking out, thinking the world is coming to an end. Then the guy comes out and tells me he's going to release me because my mom had agreed to handle it from there. I'm thinking, whew, thank you God!

That was a big mistake. Because when I got inside the house, my mom did handle it. For several days thereafter, I had my regrets. It would have been a lot less painful to my backside if I had gone to juvie hall like the policeman had threatened.

After eighth grade I petitioned the school administration to allow me to make an out-of-district move and attend Jefferson High School, partially because my dad had opened a restaurant near there. But all my friends went to Jefferson's biggest rival, Grant. It was an eye-opening experience for me because, for the first time in my life, I got exposed to a world outside my friendly little community. Now I was the outsider. Worse than that, I was the agitator on the Sabin team that had beat up on all those student athletes at the neighboring schools. Now most of those "losers" had been funneled into Jefferson High, and when they learned one of the hated Bombers was on their campus, they exacted their revenge. I didn't realize there was so much animosity and jealousy over athletics at the grade school and junior-high levels, but I found out soon enough.

The first day of classes I got pushed around by an upperclassman while we were in line to get our library cards. That guy pushed the wrong dude because my demeanor at the time was I wouldn't let stuff slide. I had this big ol' biology book in my hand and I proceeded to bounce it off the top of his head. I think that was probably the only time I ever used the biology book.

The balance of my high school career was a blur, except for basketball. That's where I excelled. First as a freshman playing for Jefferson—where I won every game against Grant, the school my old Sabin teammates all attended. And then for Grant—where I transferred after I had been "disinvited" by Jefferson administrators. My dad had closed his restaurant by then, but I think it had more to do with the number of fights I had in ninth grade.

I was reunited with my friends at Grant High School, and I reveled in the fact as a sophomore I led our junior varsity basketball team to victories over Jefferson. From then on I figured I was the X-factor, the player who could turn losers into winners. The problem was I failed to put an emphasis on my studies. I treated school as a social event, a place to play sports and meet girls. School for me at that time was still a matter of inconvenience; I only went so I could play sports. I used to cut classes all the time. We would go in the bathroom and smoke weed. Plus, you roll a few joints and then you get the girls because they want to get high.

Scholastically, I just drifted through my junior year. But on the court my desire and physical capabilities made me successful. I had sprouted to six-foot-four, and although I didn't bulk up until my senior year, I was a competitive problem for the opposition. I also had a big mouth and a quick wit, which usually got me into trouble for talking trash.

I finally met my match on the basketball floor when Grant played Benson, the eventual state champion in 1973. Jumping center for the Engineers—now the Techmen—was six-foot-nine Richard Washington, arguably the greatest high school basketball player to ever come out of Oregon. When I reached out to shake hands with the all-star at the beginning of the game, Richard punked me by first sticking his hand out—and then withdrawing it. It was a prank older brothers would often play on their younger siblings. Nobody but the two of us knew it, but Richard Washington and I were actually brothers. We had seen each other a couple of times over the years, but that jump ball was the first time we had faced off on the court. Even though it was insults and slights like the one Richard pulled on me that triggered the intensity of my athletic competition, our Grant team was overmatched, and my older brother's team won handily.

I vowed the next year would be different. Richard had graduated after leading Benson to two state championships and was playing for UCLA and its legendary coach, John Wooden. Benson was still ranked number one, but Grant was a close second. Me and everyone else at Grant had high expectations for the city championship, but those hopes were dashed when I was declared academically ineligible and missed all but the final three games of the season.

In my mind, I was thinking since I'm the star player on the team, I don't have to go to school. What are they going to do? Flunk me? Uh, yeah. While the other teachers were letting me slide with a "C-" or a "D+," my history teacher, Miss Rudy, failed me for missing too many classes. My charges of racism fell on deaf ears in the principal's office. Even though I thought Miss Rudy was the wicked witch of the East and a racist neo-Nazi, I realized later she was the best thing that ever happened to me.

Getting booted off the basketball team my senior year was my wake-up call to the reality of life. Sports had been the only thing that mattered to me, but from then on I benefited from learning the lesson there was a cost associated with enjoying the privilege of participating in something that gives you so much joy. The promise of rejoining the team—as soon as I got my grade point average up—provided ample motivation for me to refocus on my studies. I attacked the books as if my life depended on it. And in a way it did. Because if I didn't get my grades up, I wouldn't graduate. And if that happened, my mother would surely kill me.

My hard work in the classroom paid off and I rejoined the team for the league championship tournament. I had a great first game, as we easily beat Washington in the first round. That gave me my swagger back. The day of the game against second-round opponent, Adams, me and some of my teammates strutted over to their campus in a show of bravado. We talked smack to some of the players, promising a Grant victory later that evening.

That's always been part of my persona, making sure my opponent knows I'm the one who is going to kick his ass. One of my favorite nicknames was "The Prophet" because, à la Muhammad Ali, I would predict victory with boastful pre-game taunts like, "I'm the prophet, baby. I'm telling you we're going to beat you, so when you get beat you know it wasn't no accident." That day, when I spied Adams' big guy in the cafeteria, I walked right up to him and introduced myself as the one who was going to deliver the whuppin'. Several hours later I did just that.

But we lost in the championship game against Benson. I didn't find out until years later some of my teammates weren't too happy I had been getting all the glory for our playoff run, so they wanted to make sure I didn't have another big game. But the jealousy conspiracy backfired, and my high school days ended with a loss.

After that, my trash-talking opponents called me the "False Prophet." My team had been picked to win the state championship, but we didn't even make it out of our own league playoffs. With my piss-poor grades and cruel end to my high school basketball career, I figured I could kiss goodbye my dream of getting a scholarship to play college basketball, at least Division I ball. And that probably meant I wouldn't be following in my big brother's footsteps, which would lead him to the NBA. That thought frightened me. I had no idea what I was going to do after high school if I couldn't play sports.

I did get a few letters of interest from schools like the University of Oregon and Montana State, but they all said the same thing: "Go to community college and get your grades up; then give us a call." The one JC that showed the most interest offered both me and my Sabin Bomber basketball buddy, Steve Alexander, a scholarship. Even though I had no idea where Spokane, Washington, was, I accepted the offer to play basketball at Spokane Community College.

It made my parents proud their son would be going to college. But sadly, my dad would never see me play for Spokane. The day before I was to leave—with two of my new coaches at the house to ensure nothing went wrong at the last minute—dad had a heart attack and died. I was only seventeen. My dad had just retired. And my mom had health issues. I told the coaches to go on home. I wouldn't be attending their school. After the funeral, I told my mom of my decision to stay home and take care of her.

"The hell you ain't going to school," I remember her yelling. "Boy, I appreciate you being sensitive, but I was taking care of myself before you was around, and I'll be taking care of myself now. You standing around here ain't going to bring him back alive."

Arguing the point with my mother was futile. So I packed my belongings into my 1964 Ford Falcon in search of Spokane, Washington, some 350 miles northeast of Portland. When I found the school, it was everything I imagined it would be: lily white, with the only African Americans on campus part of the basketball team. It was the first time I had been away from home on my own. I was not yet eighteen years old, very immature, and totally lost.

I didn't fit in, which exacerbated my insecurities. So I took out my frustrations on the court against my teammates and coaches. Only weeks into my freshman year, my head coach pulled me aside after a particularly rowdy practice. I thought I was about to be kicked off the team for my bad behavior. I was such a rebel, such a difficult person to be around. I didn't have any mature adult around who would slap me upside the head and talk some sense into me.

But that's essentially what Coach Johnson did. He counseled me about

Playing for the Sasquatches in Spokane, #33 was described as "one of the best of the best."

the wisdom of trying to get my teammates to like me, not fear me. Coach told me I didn't always have to come across as the tough guy. And then he built me up by telling me I had the potential to become one of the best players on the team. That kind of gave me a big head. As I redirected my aggressive play to the opposing players, I helped lead the team to a record twenty-two-win season. And my head seemingly swelled with every victory.

Everybody knew my name

because I was often featured in the local media. Everybody, including the cops, who knew me better as the incorrigible violator of local speed limit laws. As the Big Man on Campus, I guessed wrongly I was immune to the punishment that accompanied unpaid speeding tickets. The twelfth one ignored and crumpled in my glove box proved to be the last straw.

I got hauled in on a warrant for my arrest one Friday afternoon, and because I was so ashamed and embarrassed to call someone and make bail, I spent the entire weekend sitting and sleeping on a bench in a filthy shared holding cell. I was the only black man in that small contained space, with a bunch of drunks and crazy people. I didn't eat anything. I didn't drink anything. And I didn't bathe. But I did win at least one fight while in the tank. Come Monday morning when I appeared before a judge, I looked a mess—and about six pounds lighter.

The judge, apparently a big Sasquatch fan—Sasquatch was our team name and I probably resembled our mascot after that long weekend—let me know everyone missed watching me play Saturday night. "And by the way, your team lost without you there," he told me with obvious disappointment in his voice.

The basketball junkie judge chastised me for my apparent lack of respect for the law, but he wiped out my fines in lieu of the miserable time already served. Plus, he offered some career advice, which I smartly took: get rid of the car.

I valued my shot at becoming a professional basketball player more than I did racing that dinged-up Ford Falcon, so I parted ways with it. The other lesson that stuck with me after that weekend in the slammer was my vow never to do anything that would cause me to spend one more minute in a jail cell.

With me back on the team, we made it all the way to the championship game. But in an unfortunate twist of fate, the day before the tournament was to start, déjà vu happened all over again and thwarted my chance of winning a championship. Two of our best players got kicked off the team for trying to steal a television. Outmanned, we lost the championship game. Same result the following year. It appeared my basketball-playing days were over.

If I had only known about the letters, I might have hit the big time. Apparently, Coach Johnson really wanted me on his squad the full two years. So he never told me about the recruiting letters he intercepted after my stellar first year. From several Division I teams. And even a pro team. By the time I learned about the letters of interest, it was too late. At the time, it bothered me greatly, and I promised never to set foot on the SCC campus again. It took me thirty-five years to get over that slight, but when both my teams were elected to Spokane Community College's Hall of Fame, I accepted the invitation to attend the induction ceremony. I brought my family and they got to hear Coach Johnson cite my many top-ten school records and praise me as "one of the best of the best."

I thought my college basketball career was over, but there was still a chance I wasn't done playing. During my two years in Spokane, I had made quite an impression on the coach of Gonzaga University's basketball team. I often practiced with the Zags, whose gym was just a short drive from SCC, and, in my humble opinion, I was better than their big men. A scholarship offer was in the works, so I kept practicing with Gonzaga and stayed in Spokane during the negotiations. I was even invited to play in the team's summer tournament in Southern California. But then I received the message that changed all that.

As our team was preparing for the trip, I got a phone call from my uncle, my mother's brother. Uncle Garfield had never called me before, so I surmised something bad must have happened. I was devastated by the news my mother had just undergone brain surgery to remove a tumor. I was terrified, I mean, it scared the crap out of me. I can't lose my mom. We just lost my dad, and if I lose my mother I got nobody.

I desperately tried to reach my mom, but all the hospital would tell me was she had the operation and was in recovery. I knew I couldn't stay put.

And there was no way I was going to California. I needed to get home. Now! When I explained the situation to the Gonzaga coach, the response was less than sympathetic. In fact, the man's words were quite heartless. He basically told me to man up, accompany the team on their afternoon flight, and then go home to my mommy after the tournament. That hit me like a ton of bricks. That guy didn't give a crap about me.

And at that moment I didn't care about the coach, the players, Southern California, or even basketball. All I was focused on was getting back to Portland the fastest way possible. In my hand were my round-trip airline tickets, voucher for the hotel, and my meal tickets. But as the rest of the team filed onto the plane at Spokane International Airport, I hung back. After everyone else was on board, I turned around, walked back to the counter, and exchanged my ticket for a one-way trip to Portland International—impossible now, but doable in 1976. I was going home to take care of Mom.

CHAPTER SIX

Transformation of a Goofy-Footer

Growing up in Orange County, California, in the 1960s was like living in an insulated bubble, a very white bubble. We used to joke that anyone who drove through that area back then would have needed sunglasses "because of all the whiteness of the people." It was also right-winged, anti-communist, and anti-government. This I learned from my dad, who got his marching orders from reading the ultra-conservative *The Blue Book* of the John Birch Society. Or Dad's polarized opinions could have been gleaned from the daily newspaper, the *Santa Ana Register,* whose conservative editorials he read religiously.

Much like my tidy life at Alpenrose, I felt shielded from a lot of the divisive issues most of America seemed to be dealing with in the sixties, particularly civil rights and racism. Shoot, we lived blocks away from Disneyland's Fantasyland—the magical place where reality was up for interpretation and you felt insulated from the real world outside. As for my dealing with people of another color, there were quite a few Hispanics in Orange County, but there had been zero black kids at John

C. Fremont Jr. High. And among the more than 2,000 students who attended Anaheim Union High School, only two were African American—brothers from one family. What knowledge I scraped together about the plight of blacks in America I learned from watching television or reading a newspaper other than the *Santa Ana Register*.

Now, I'm sure I thought civil rights was proper and correct and right, and they shouldn't be beating those black people on the TV news. And they definitely shouldn't shoot Medgar Evers or bomb the church where those four little black girls got killed. It was wrong. It was bad. But it didn't really affect us. We didn't march. We went surfing.

Even after the tragic assassination of President John F. Kennedy, there was this cultural malaise that seemed to settle like a protective blanket over Anaheim, somehow segregating the locals and their "Bircher mentality" from feeling the pain the rest of America experienced. I was just as callous. Our classes were canceled and teachers encouraged all of us students to go to area churches and pray. Before taking advantage of that free day off, I felt compelled to mark the historic event by using a pocketknife to carve my name on the underside of a desk, along with the note, "JFK was killed this day in November." Then me and my surfing friends did a "pray-by" past the local Catholic Church on our way to the beach.

Our reactions to the Watts riots in Los Angeles two years later—where thirty-four people were killed over six days of racially fueled violence—were similarly uncaring. Sure, we watched it on TV, but my feelings of white indifference, which I didn't identify with until decades later, caused me to basically turn off the television and go surfing. My foolish reaction, which had been engrained in me, was the typical white guy's response: "Hey, I didn't cause the riots. I didn't do it! Doesn't have anything to do with me." So, me and my friends, we drive south to Doheny, to Dana Point. We don't go north to Watts because that's where the black people are rioting.

Surfing continued to dominate my almost daily routine through high school graduation, but once freed up from the constraints of my studies I embraced another habit—getting high with my friends. I had moved out of the Pancake House and into an apartment in Newport Beach with some buddies. One night at a party somebody lit up a joint and passed it around. I was probably drunk and so I smoked it. I liked it, thought it was better than getting drunk.

At first, I told myself I would only smoke marijuana if someone else had it and offered it to me. After a while I convinced myself to buy my own, but only enough for one day's supply. That didn't last too long, so I compromised and told myself I would buy just enough to last a few days. But I drew the line at selling the stuff. Eventually I crossed that line, too, investing in larger quantities and selling enough to cover my expenses.

That escalation took a dangerous turn when I participated in a drug deal south of the border. I knew it was a risky venture, so instead of driving my own car into Mexico, I borrowed my dad's Cadillac for the run. A drug dealer named Danny rode shotgun and funded the buy—$350 for fourteen kilos (about thirty pounds). The rumor was the Tijuana dope peddlers would tip off the border guards by giving them the license plate numbers of the gringo buyers, so me and Danny conspired with another guy to transfer the bundles of marijuana into his car. That driver got to keep a kilo for his role. I got one for doing my part, and Danny sold the rest at three times what he paid for it.

Now, I was smart enough not to try something so dangerous and foolish again, but that didn't stop me from experimenting with harder drugs. I even tried mescaline one night with my friend, Ernie, but immediately after we had snorted the hallucinogenic powder we got nose bleeds. It was strange, because the blood seemed to be dripping out of my nose in slow motion and creating this puddle on the table. The thought, of course, was, "I'm having a good time. This is fun!" But then I distinctly remembered thinking, "Do I have to get this messed up just to live?"

That revelation prompted me to start thinking seriously about what I was going to do with my life. By then I was making three dollars an hour working weekends at the Pancake House. During the week I surfed. I had started taking classes at Fullerton Junior College, but bounced around, declaring four or five different majors during the three years it took me to earn a two-year Associate of Arts degree. I liked my political science classes the most, particularly the notion of helping the underdog and advocating for social change. So it wasn't that surprising—at least to my friends—the first cause I fought for was the legalization of pot. I couldn't even hide my pro-marijuana stance because my picture was featured in the April 23, 1967, issue of the *Los Angeles Times* during a student rally at Fullerton JC. Under the photo of me wearing dark sunglasses was the caption, "Student Wendell Birkland raises a point on a discussion of drugs and narcotics." Of course, I was stoned at the time.

What's odd is I didn't realize back then where marijuana would take me. It took me to a point where everything is okay. Well, if marijuana's okay, then hashish is okay. And if hashish is okay, LSD must be okay. If LSD is okay, then mescaline is okay. And if we can find anything else, that's okay, too. I believe that's the delusion of the enemy. And in the midst of that, everything was okay. Lying to your mother's okay. Deceiving women is okay to get what you want. I remember thinking lying is wrong—*I knew it was wrong*—but I got to the point where I didn't care. I even became proud of how well I could lie.

My life had been trailing away from God ever since I chickened out of acknowledging him as a twelve-year-old. I rarely went to church anymore. I was drinking more. Smoking more. Just drifting down a road that seemed doomed. And then for a period of time I was just downright angry at God. I got a call at work one afternoon informing me my favorite youth pastor—Roy Mourer—had died of a heart attack. He was the Camp Crestview leader who had won so many souls for Jesus and I loved him. I was crying and all pissed off at God. I remember screaming, "Why in the world would you kill this guy? He's serving you and I'm living for the enemy! He's dead and I'm alive. This is crazy!" Then the strangest thing happened. I got an answer from God; I truly felt like I heard his voice. He said, "Roy was ready; you're not."

I would like to say I immediately fell on my face and surrendered my life to him, but I didn't. I just carried on with my worldly ways. I did have a girlfriend who attended Bible college and once in a while I would go to church with her. But otherwise I had no direction, no plan for the rest of my life.

I finally chose a career path when a counselor told me I could parlay a degree in political science into three jobs—work for the State Department, teach political science, or become a lawyer. I didn't like the first two choices, so I decided to become a lawyer. History is strange, you know, because I ended up in a career working on criminal cases. I mean, I was a criminal. I had a criminal mind. In my heart, at least, I had violated each of the Ten Commandments. I didn't murder anybody, but there was a time I hated my dad.

After I determined to study law, I knew it was time to focus on getting better grades. I made the Dean's List at Cal State Fullerton my last semester. Now all that stood between me and acceptance at a law school was the Law School Admission Test. I knew that many students opted for the LSAT prep course to learn how to take the test. But my preparation was different—I didn't smoke any dope the night before the test. But I did take two joints with me, cuz I figured I'd need them for the drive back from Riverside.

I ended up passing the test. And my grades were good enough to get accepted at Willamette University College of Law in Salem, Oregon. Looking back, I can't even imagine how God protected me. There I was with my acceptance to Willamette; I'm almost graduated, I was surfing and hanging out, getting loaded…and my whole thought process was how could I put aside money to buy enough weed and hash and pills to take with me to Oregon so I wouldn't have to make a purchase from somebody in Salem I didn't trust. *What in the world was I thinking?!*

I realize my reasoning was delusional at the time. But even with my acceptance letter in hand and a promising future within my grasp, I continued to make bonehead decisions that jeopardized my prospects. My vision of becoming a lawyer almost flitted away when my mom found some hash I had been storing in the Pancake House—and threatened to call the police.

Now, I realize I should have been concerned that my mother had found my contraband and was running around the house screaming, but my only concern at the moment was whether she had found the rest of the hash I had hidden elsewhere—just in case someone found the one stash, the other wouldn't be in jeopardy. I was relieved to learn she had only confiscated half my supply, but the relief turned to terror when Mom told me she was going to turn me in. With my law degree in limbo, I pleaded my case. I told my mother if she called the police I could end up with a felony and that would destroy my career.

I thought it was a good sell, you know, a classic closing argument. As far as I knew, she didn't make the call. But years later she told me she actually had called to report me. The thing that's kind of miraculous is she couldn't get through. She said she called the emergency 911 number and could not get through. If she had gotten through to the authorities, I wouldn't have ever become a lawyer.

But that near-miss didn't interfere with my short-term plans. In less than six weeks, I would be moving to Oregon and starting law school, so I needed to get my act together. I had already made up my mind I was going to continue using drugs for recreational purposes, but since I didn't know anybody in Salem to buy from, I determined to build up my inventory for the trip north. So I went about making plans, mentally filling my back-to-school shopping cart with one kilo of marijuana, three or four ounces of hash, and an assortment of psychedelic pills. That should tide me over to the second semester, I deduced. Certainly by then I expected I would have met some trustworthy fellows who could become my new suppliers.

Moving back to Oregon meant I would be living less than an hour's drive away from my grandparents. I had been gone for more than ten years and was looking forward to returning to Alpenrose, a place that held many fond memories for me. I also thought it would be a good idea to provide them with regular updates on my studies because Grandma and Grandpa had offered to support me through law school. Unbeknownst to me at the time, Grandma Cadonau was providing more than financial support—she was on her knees daily with spiritual support, praying I would get right with Jesus. She would call me almost every Saturday, asking if I was doing okay, was I going to church tomorrow, sweet stuff like that.

I don't remember if it was my grandmother's constant cajoling or my girlfriend's persistent invitations, but, for some reason on a Sunday shortly before I was to leave my California life behind, I went with my girlfriend to Lake Avenue Church in Pasadena. As was my custom—it was little over an hour's drive, after all—I smoked two joints on the way. And, in my full flamboyant fashion, I entered the conservative house of worship wearing my shades; a very bright green, red, and yellow Hawaiian shirt; white bellbottoms; and sandals.

But I got sober real quick when the pastor began his sermon about how the loose-living culture of the day was in direct opposition to the Ten Commandments. As he ticked off each Commandment—and the corresponding example of society's current lifestyle that violated it—I felt extreme guilt. As I sank lower and lower in the pew, I felt the preacher was speaking directly to me, as if nobody else was in the sanctuary. And based on his interpretation of what I had just heard, I hadn't violated merely one or two of God's laws: I was guilty of disobeying all of them. My conviction was sealed when the pastor finished up by saying the only way to make things right with God was to repent and ask for forgiveness.

I left that church convinced I needed to make some major changes in my life. When I woke up the next morning—Monday, July 28th—I realized in exactly thirty days I would be starting classes at Willamette. Throughout that day, as I surfed and hung out with my same friends, I couldn't shake the preacher's convicting words. I desperately wanted the peace the man promised would be mine if I would just surrender my life to Christ. Memories of rejecting that peace when I was twelve haunted me.

I remember taking my girlfriend to a movie in Hollywood that night, but I paid little attention to the big screen. In my mind I couldn't stop replaying the terrible things I had done in my life, the people I had hurt, the laws I had broken. By the time we got back to my girlfriend's place, I was overcome by my sense of guilt and sorrow. When she asked what was wrong, the floodgates opened. I began to weep uncontrollably...for what seemed like an hour. I begged for God's forgiveness. And while it felt kind of strange in front of my girlfriend, I knew I had to do it—I began to confess both audibly and silently the sins of my life up to that time.

After I repented I prayed to receive Jesus. Then I got up off the floor, wiped my tears away, and ran to the telephone to call my grandmother. I apparently had lost track of time—it was after one in the morning when I dialed her number—so it took a long while for her to answer. But when I told her what had just happened, she was elated—her prayers had been answered!

My roommate, Ernie, wasn't exactly thrilled when I got home and woke him up in the middle of the night to tell him about my encounter with God. And he became downright angry when I started flushing our drugs down the toilet. But this time I wouldn't be sidetracked. I had less than thirty days to confess Jesus. My plan was to let all my friends know I had become a born-again Christian. Well, my announcement was met with less than enthusiasm at Dick Williams'

Grandma Cadonau was a spiritual mentor to me over the years, even when I strayed.

house where Neal and some of the boys were hanging out and getting high. By this time, I had sworn off drugs and I was trying to explain to the guys how God had changed my ways, that I was a different person now. The only reaction was from some hippie dude who, through a haze of marijuana smoke, yelled, "Far out! Birkland's on a religious trip. Somebody pass me another joint!"

I realized, in short order, this wasn't going to have the impact I'd hoped for. My conversion wasn't exactly received with gladness and joy by my friends. But that didn't stop me from telling everybody what I believed and what I felt God was doing in my life. It was very important to me because I didn't want to fall into the same trap I fell into as a twelve-year-old. I never again wanted to be guilty of being ashamed of Jesus.

Radical. That's how everyone perceived my transformation. My parents were happy to learn I was straightening out my life, but my friends were nonplussed. I tried one last time to share Jesus with my buddies at a typical Friday night drug and alcohol–fueled party, but when one of the guys who was high on something greeted me at the door on all fours, barking like a dog, I determined I couldn't deal with crazy. So I moved on. I didn't give up surfing, but the vices that had dominated my "California experience" no longer controlled me.

I was anxious to start my new life afresh back in Oregon. I had found a small place to rent in a four-plex not far from campus and plunked down $510 for one year's rent. Then I packed all my stuff in a van and moved to Salem. I didn't know anyone at Willamette University, so I figured a clever way to meet people would be to start a Bible study group. When my constitutional law professor allowed me to make an announcement at the end of class one Monday morning, I took the microphone and addressed the 150 or so students:

"Good morning, my name is Wendell Birkland and I'm a Christian, a follower of Jesus, you know, and I'm going to start a Bible study if anybody is interested. So please see me after class and we can talk about getting together."

As I stood by, all 150 students filed out the door without as much as a word. Well, at least I had some old friends at Portland Foursquare Church. That became my spiritual and social hangout every Sunday. Of course, I looked forward to sitting next to my grandparents for morning services, but I also had my eye on a certain young woman who, since I had been gone, had blossomed from a seven-year-old kid into a seven-teen-year-old beauty. I was six years older than Kristi Lee and knew her family well because the Birklands and the Lees were longtime friends from church. But it wasn't until two years earlier, when the Lee family had visited us on their annual summer vacation to California, that I had *really* begun to notice her. I had only been back in Oregon a few months, and even though we hadn't yet gone out on a date, glances had been exchanged every Sunday and I knew there was a mutual attraction. That was con-firmed around Christmas 1969 when, after church, I was in my Porsche stopped at a red light and Kristi pulled up next to me. She got so flustered when our eyes met she drove right through the red light. A cop behind her flipped his lights on and pulled her over. I waved as I drove by, confident we would become an item. When I went back to Anaheim over Christmas break I told the old girlfriend I wouldn't be marrying her.

Kristi Lee was crowned Queen of the Portland Rose Festival in 1971. We got married in 1973.

Back in Oregon, my friendship with Kristi began to develop over soft drinks after church. She was a junior at Roosevelt High and that year was named Queen of the Portland Rose Festival Court. Her senior year she went to the prom with the class presi-dent, but after graduation the two of us began an exclusive relationship.

I was a third-year law student when she enrolled at Willamette. That year, instead of only weekend visits as before, we enjoyed seeing each other practically every day. I was already interning at the Multnomah County District Attorney's office in Portland, and it was my goal to get a full-time job there so I could ask Kristi to marry me. I got hired as Deputy DA a few weeks after I passed the Oregon State Bar exam, and we got married shortly thereafter.

In retrospect, my three-year makeover was quite remarkable—from drugged-out surfer dude pancake flipper to a respectable married man prosecuting drug crimes for the District Attorney. I was reading the Bible, attending church, and growing in my Christian faith. After we married, Kristi and I began teaching Sunday school—first for junior high school kids and later for adult classes—at Portland Foursquare, a passion we shared for more than fifteen years. We purchased our first house—a 900-square-foot starter home in Southwest Portland we got for $15,000. I was actually shopping for what we newlyweds could afford—the absolute cheapest house listed by the Regional Multiple Listing Service—but we ended up with the second cheapest home in the area because someone else beat us to the fixer-upper priced at $11,500. We cashed in a savings bond I had been given as a young child to make the down payment.

I loved my new job as a rookie Deputy District Attorney. I became as passionate for the work as I had been with surfing, approaching my role as a prosecuting trial lawyer like I did the swells at Lower Trestles—meeting the challenges head-on, wave after wave. My first assignment was the drug unit, a place where I felt moderately comfortable given my huge investment of time and resources into California's drug culture. I certainly understood the perpetrator's point of view. I excelled at putting the bad guys behind bars, so they moved me to the busier assault and robbery unit. After a year, I got an appointment to Circuit Court Deputy, which meant I could try felony cases. Two years into that role, my boss, District Attorney Michael Schrunk, added me to the homicide sex crimes unit and began piling on the workload with murder cases.

I was just working my tail off and loving every minute of it. My boss always said he exploited me, but I proved to him I could absorb the work. I had a strong work ethic and wanted to try as many murder cases as I could. And I got just what I wanted.

I figure forty murder cases crossed my desk in a two-year period. Most were what I would call "run-of-the-mill" murders, but there were some memorable ones. Like Timmy Thurston who robbed taverns on Thursdays. Timmy pulled his last weekly heist with his brother, and they ended up shooting and killing someone. I successfully prosecuted both of them. In another win, as soon as the judge proclaimed a guilty verdict, the African-American man I was prosecuting bolted from the courtroom and I ran after him. As I chased the guy through Lownsdale Park, across from the courthouse, I remembered thinking, "Hey, this guy is bigger, stronger, and faster than me. What could I really do if I were to catch him?" I gave up the chase after recalling there'd been testimony the runner was a brown belt in karate.

I had never been comfortable with violence as a kid, but two years prosecuting murderers, rapists, and other dangerous criminals steeled me to the point where I could enjoy the battle. I didn't like the ugliness associated with trying violent offenders, but my motivation to win—fueled by my fear of dropping the ball and losing a case—toughened me. Plus, I was very good at my job, even though it was common knowledge you never lose in the DA's office; you had to really screw up for someone to be found not guilty. People told me I had a sharp wit, the intellect, and the verbal skills needed to sway judges and jurors in my favor. My sense is I simply outworked most of my opponents.

But after a while what I lacked was the challenge. Rubber stamping guilty verdicts in murder case after murder case became mundane—the commentary around the DA's office was akin to "they're all guilty; we just haven't found them all yet." I was carrying the biggest load of the three prosecuting attorneys in the homicide unit—who all made the same $640-a-month salary—and that wasn't getting me anywhere but burned out. By that time, Kristi and I had two children and we had outgrown our tiny starter home. I had to figure out a way to make more money because working like a deputy dog for the county wasn't providing the financial resources our growing family needed. I had always been interested in going into private practice, so when another lawyer in the district attorney's office approached me about going into business for ourselves, I jumped at the chance. After spending four years prosecuting law breakers, I switched sides, and with my new associate, Dale, started the criminal defense firm, Birkland & Koch.

CHAPTER SEVEN

Salvation

The doctors gave my mom a fifty-percent chance of surviving the brain surgery. They told me they wouldn't know for at least six months if she would make it because that's when they would go back in and see if they had gotten all of the tumor. In my mind, all I heard was my mother's going to die. I thought I was going to lose her; it felt like my whole world was coming to an end.

It wasn't my biggest worry at that moment, but it sure looked like my basketball career was over. The last my prospective Gonzaga teammates saw of me was my backside when I bolted from the terminal as they were boarding the plane to Southern California. I was in such a hurry to be with my mom in Portland I left all my belongings in Spokane. And when I got home my worst fears were realized. My own mother, with her head swollen and bandaged, barely recognized me. She was only fifty-four years old, but she was so sick and feeble I was terrified I was going to lose her. I stayed by her side, watching over her, as she slowly recovered.

When I felt comfortable enough to take a moment to consider my own future, I got worried again. Phone calls from the coaches and teammates at Gonzaga University went unanswered, until they stopped calling altogether. So that door—the only one that might have led to a career as a professional basketball player—was closed. When I abandoned Spokane Community College, I left without a degree or good enough grades to transfer to a four-year school, so my chances of ever graduating from college were south of slim-to-none. I didn't have a car. And I had left most of my clothes back at the dorm. Plus, I didn't have a job. Which meant I didn't have any money. As I wallowed in my sad situation, I came to the realization I really had nothing. Not even hope.

But one day "hope" tracked me down. My salvation came in the form of a phone call from the mother of my friend, Greg. With my mom on the mend, I had moved into a two-bedroom apartment with a buddy, and then I invited my girlfriend from Spokane to join me. One afternoon when I was at the apartment by myself, the phone rang. It was Mrs. McDonald, whom I considered my second mom. As close as we were growing up, this was the first time in my life Mrs. McDonald had ever called me on the phone. And to this day I can't figure out how she got my number.

She had my number alright. Barely past hello, this loving Christian woman had a pointed question for me: "Larry, do you know Jesus?"

My lame answer—that I went to church—did not deter her from her mission.

"Yes, Larry," she patiently replied. "I know you go to church, but do you have Jesus Christ in your life?"

Mrs. McDonald then proceeded to lay out God's plan of salvation, which involved repenting of my sins and inviting Jesus to be Lord of my life. She got me to acknowledge that my lifestyle—particularly the new living arrangement with my girlfriend—was not right. I don't know how long we talked, but finally when she asked if we could pray together that I would receive Jesus in my heart, I said yes. So she said this prayer on the phone and led me to accept Jesus Christ as my Lord and Savior.

After a few "Hallelujahs," "Praise Jesus," and "Thank you Lord," Mrs. McDonald hung up the phone. I could hardly believe what had just happened—did I really just get saved over the phone? It was confirmed when my roommate got home from work and asked what was new. I told him I think I just discovered Jesus.

In the morning there was no question left in my mind. I had had an encounter with Jesus. My conversion was real. And I felt convicted to make some immediate changes in my life. Mrs. McDonald, bless her heart, was right...about a lot of things. For the first time, I truly felt God's presence with me. I felt loved. And I got back what I had lost—hope for the future. But as I packed my bags to move back in with my mom, I knew Mrs. McDonald was right about my promiscuous lifestyle. It was not a pleasant conversation, but I was adamant I needed to sever my relationship with the live-in girlfriend. I also felt compelled to make amends with people I had ripped off or conned along the way. That meant returning my only mode of transportation—a bicycle I had taken off a neighboring porch.

Mrs. McDonald encouraged me, as a new believer, to read the Bible and learn as much as I could about what it meant to be a follower of Jesus. She also invited me to study under the tutelage of her husband, Curtis "Brother Mac" McDonald, who operated what he called "Open Book Bible Study" out of his office. I brought the same intensity to Bible study that I had carried with me on the basketball court. I became a voracious reader and note taker who regularly kept Brother Mac up late into the night with questions about my new-found faith.

Over time, my life was transformed from Larry, "the new believer," to Larry, "the knower." I didn't simply believe Jesus would do what he said he would, I absolutely knew it from the bottom of my heart. I was convinced—as I learned from my readings—that Jesus Christ is the same yesterday and today and forever. And that meant miracles were possible.

One night while I was staying at my mom's, I heard her downstairs, just moaning and groaning in pain. I'd been reading in the Bible where it says if you pray to God, he will hear you. So my prayer was like, "God, I'm really scared; it's my mom, and I don't know what to do. Please help me!"

Right then and there, in my upstairs bedroom, I felt God told me to go downstairs to my mother's bedroom, put my hands on her head, and claim her healing in the name of Jesus. Just like that! So I got up, went downstairs, walked into my mother's room—which is something I never did—and she had this surprised look on her face. I reached down and put my hands on her head. I think I was scared, and I might have scared her, too; but I grabbed her head and held it. Then I said, "In the name of Jesus, you are healed!"

It was awkward. And embarrassing. In fact, I felt so stupid I ran out of the room and raced back up the stairs to my bedroom. Me and Mom never talked about the supernatural incident. Not when she turned sixty years old. Or seventy. Or eighty. Or even when she celebrated her 97th birthday in 2017.

You can't tell me God isn't real. He healed my mother. And he healed me, too. That day he changed a scared little boy who didn't know anything, didn't know enough not to believe God could do a miracle on his mother. That moment was the beginning of my walk with him in a real way, not a superficial religious way, not some intellectual or knowledge way, but in a personal way. He did this for me.

I was on fire for the Lord—fanatical, some might have said.

A brain tumor gave my mom a 50-50 chance of surviving. She lived to be 97.

People who knew me as "that bully crazy dude who used to chase people" now recognized me as "that Bible-totin' Jesus freak who used to be that bully crazy dude who chased people." With Bible in hand, and dressed in a suit and tie, I would evangelize in my neighborhood, on the city bus that got me to and from school, even at Portland Community College where I was taking some classes. I hung out with a group of like-minded people in the cafeteria and we would have these lunch discussions about different topics from the Bible. We even formed an on-campus club—we called it Christian Fellowship. It was kind of funny: some twenty years later when I was a recruiter for the police bureau, I was back on that campus and I sat in on a meeting of the Christian Fellowship Club. I had long since forgot about it, but it was still going on. It was just another confirmation for me that God is real, that his word is faithful.

Life was good for me in my early twenties. I had participated in my mother's miraculous healing and helped nurse her back to a full recovery. I was secure in my faith as a follower of Jesus. I was earning straight A's as a part-time student at Portland Community College. And I was playing basketball at a very high level in a summer league called Portland Pro-Am. I was one of the organizers along with my brother, Richard, and my good friend, Donald Dixon. We eventually got affiliated with the NBA and attracted lots of professionals like Terry Porter, Michael Holton, Jerome Kersey, and Kevin Duckworth. I was part of it for more than ten years—and if they would have given out rings for every championship I would have one on every finger. Pro-Am really fulfilled a big need in my life to compete. And it was personally satisfying because for years I had the camaraderie of a great group of guys.

But I couldn't ignore the fact I had no prospects for a job, much less a career. And it was time I moved out on my own.

I was contemplating such things one afternoon sitting on my mom's front porch. While thoughts like "I don't want to work at McDonald's," and "But you don't got a whole lot of skill; you don't have much education," were ruminating in my mind, a patrol car slowed down in front of the house. And the cop shined his spotlight on me. In broad daylight.

I remember thinking, "What the heck? Why you eyeballing me? Yeah, I'm black. And I'm sitting here on my porch. I must be a suspect, right?" That was my first reaction. And then I had another thought: "There's something I can do. I like guns. I can be violent. I can pass the drug test. I haven't gotten in any real trouble. You know what? I can probably do that."

The more I thought about becoming a police officer, the more I liked the idea. But the notion almost got derailed when I told my mother. My mom, you would have thought I told her I had decided to be a woman. She was like, "I absolutely do not want you to do that!"

I tried to be a good son, and so I tolerated her objections for a couple of months. But eventually I did go downtown to apply for a position with the Portland Police Bureau. And I almost left without filling out an application because the unfriendly dude in Personnel was so rude to me. If it weren't for Elmer Brown, I would never have become a cop.

I don't know if that guy had a problem with me being black, but I was so offended I chucked the application in the trash can on my way out the door. But unbeknownst to me, an older cop who was on the phone had seen what had happened and came running around the counter. He put his arm around me, walked me back in, and the two of us sat down and talked. That was a pivotal moment. I was on my way out, but Elmer Brown talked me into staying.

Fortunately for me, the Portland Police Bureau offered a Law Enforcement Training program for candidates who had no experience. I spent most of 1980 as a civilian riding around with experienced cops and pushing paper in the Central Precinct's Personnel office. The following February, I was sworn in as a member of the police force. Three other African Americans were hired then, too, the largest hiring of people of color at one time in the history of the police bureau.

It was a rough start. I failed miserably at certain administrative duties, like report writing. When a training supervisor called me out for submitting a report that "looked like a grade school kid wrote it," I repaid his disrespect by cussing him out and upending his desk in what almost progressed to fist-icuffs. "I don't know who you think you're talking to," I shouted at him. "But I am a grown man and you do not talk to me like I'm a child. If you do talk to me like a child, you better be prepared to defend yourself, because I will take this desk and throw it on top of your butt." I was certain I would be fired for my insubordination, but all I got was the silent treatment from the bosses, as well as the rank and file.

On my first day in the field with a different training coach, the officer informed me how vehemently he had objected to having to work with me. Other white officers who patrolled North and Northeast Portland expressed their distrust of a black cop working in a predominantly black neighborhood. I was big, I was athletic, and I was not afraid to share my opinion. That was very intimidating to some of my co-workers. But questioning my loyalty? That was something I resented because my loyalty, beginning when I was a kid, was always with people who were doing the right thing, even if it cost me my own friendships. I didn't think I had to choose between being a cop and being a part of my community.

When my rocky training program was finished, my North Precinct super-visors pushed me out on my own. They gave me a badge, keys to a patrol car, a shotgun, and a territory to cover. I remember putting the shotgun in the rack, the key in the ignition...and then my eyes welling up with tears. But they weren't tears of joy. I cried because I was scared to death. I was a rookie and did not have the slightest idea what I was doing. I had no clue. I am the police and I was literally terrified. I recall sitting there for a few minutes, and I told myself, "Larry, you gotta start this car up, man. You can't sit here in the garage this whole time."

I finally turned that key in the ignition, but not before considering packing up my gun and gear and dropping them off at the back door of the precinct on my way home. I was that afraid, convinced I knew nothing about police work. I was terrified I would get a call from dispatch and wouldn't know how to handle it.

And there weren't a whole lot of members of the Portland Police Bureau interested in helping out a new black officer, either, so I was stuck learning the job while performing what I hoped were the best practices of a policeman. One of my first lessons about the use of my sidearm almost got somebody killed. I was on my way back to the precinct one afternoon when I got flagged down by a crowd of people pointing out two men who were fighting. By the time I called for backup and approached the scene, one of the men had a broken bottle in his hand and was about to use it on the other guy. When the man ignored my command to put the bottle down and continued to move forward, I pulled out my gun.

I will never forget the look on that dude's face. He put the bottle down, turned toward me, and, like in slow motion, walked over to me—got right up in my face—and grabbed the end of my gun. He pulled it to his forehead and said, "Pull the trigger." Well, that ain't supposed to happen. Nobody trained me what to do if the guy doesn't stop.

So, I stared the fool down for a few seconds before I took my finger off the trigger and slowly put the weapon back in its holster. Then the crazy dude simply turned and walked off, leaving me humiliated and embarrassed in front of a bunch of snickering onlookers. The hard lesson I learned as a novice cop that day was not to be so quick to snatch your gun out of its holster because pulling guns out doesn't solve problems, it creates them.

It was a testy time for the Portland police—whether black or white. During my early tenure on the force, racial tension within the bureau spilled over into the community in two nationally embarrassing incidents for the city. Just a month into my new job, two white officers were suspended after dumping four dead opossums in front of the Burger Barn, a black-owned restaurant in Northeast Portland. Later, two other white cops were suspended for selling T-shirts with "Don't Choke 'Em, Smoke 'Em" printed on them, following a black man's death after police used a choke-hold to subdue the Marine Corps veteran during a struggle.

The welcome mat was definitely not out for me as the new recruit. The animosity I felt—from both the dominatingly white police force and my black friends who felt betrayed—made me question my decision to pursue a career as a policeman. The culture I grew up in provided reminders of the "terrorist" atrocities carried out in the past by police against blacks. It wasn't until several years into my new job I fully comprehended why my mother had pleaded with me so strongly to not become a police officer. She wasn't as worried I might be killed in the line of duty; she was afraid of what would happen to her black son in a white institution like the Portland Police Bureau.

Part of me felt staying with the bureau was a bad idea, mostly because everything about who I am culturally and as a person screamed to not go there. It was engrained in me that police are not our friends. And here I was, a black cop working in what was considered the worst community dealing every day with black-on-black crime, as well as with African Americans around crime scenes who didn't want to talk to the police because they wanted to see street justice happen. And I not only policed those streets, I lived in that community. Which is something you're never supposed to do.

Fortunately for me, before I became a cop I was well-known and respected in my community as someone who made right choices and wouldn't tolerate law breakers. Sure, I had a reputation of being a bully back in the day—a big guy on the basketball court who knocked people around a bit—but when I was in uniform, people didn't give me a whole lot of flak.

It was that exposure to the black community which made me successful in many sticky situations. Like the time I had a warrant out for this gang member who I was speaking to from a distance. The guy was fidgeting—he either had something illegal on him or he was getting ready to run. So I told him, "I see what you're doing and I know what you're thinking; seen it before. You can run—that's what the radio's for, and we'll be all over the place. But here's what you should do. I'm going to give you these handcuffs. I want you to put them on, and then I want you to walk over and get in the back of my car."

Now I was pretty sure he didn't want to be clowned in front of his friends, so when I handed him the cuffs, the kid looked around, put them on, and got into the back of my patrol car.

In those incidents—and there were many throughout my career—I believe God put me exactly where he needed me to be and I was the right guy for the right time. But even though I had become a follower of Jesus before I became a police officer, none of my fellow cops knew about my faith. That's because I never told any of them about it; and secondly, they probably wouldn't have believed me anyway because my lifestyle wasn't that different from everybody else's. Sure, I had quit drinking, but that was more of a financial decision than a spiritual one. One payday when I realized how much of my check went to buying alcohol, I just decided to stop drinking. But I still frequented the bar scene; after all, I was single and I enjoyed dancing and chasing women.

Eventually, this dual life I was living began to wear on my psyche. The barriers I had put up separating my personal life from my professional career became too many to manage. I had convinced myself my Christian faith was my own personal thing, and you didn't reveal such intimate details about yourself to people at work. But what I was really doing was living every day as if God didn't exist, as if I didn't need him. I was treating him like he was some kind of genie that showed up when you wanted him to grant you a wish.

By walling off my personal life—and faith—from the people I worked with, I had to consciously strive to keep my personality, beliefs, emotions, and feelings in check. I kept relationships at arm's length. There was little to no socializing after hours with anyone associated with the Portland Police Bureau. The problem was that policemen are out there dealing with life and death every day, and if you show up with your standoffish attitude, this "I'm-not-going-to-allow-you-into-my-life snobbishness," or some holier-than-thou bullshit, that's going to be a recipe for disaster. That's a toxic environment to be working in, especially when you are right in the mix with guys who are literally depending on you for their lives.

This period of conflict in my life unfortunately coincided with the most dangerous time in my law enforcement career. Gang activity had finally migrated from California into Oregon. Portland police had begun to see evidence of the influx, as local black kids started dressing differently and wearing the same colors as the Bloods and Crips from Los Angeles. Over a short period of time, fistfights over girls or possessions evolved into shootings over territories and drugs.

And even when I came face-to-face with this new gang presence—when a seventeen-year-old gang member regularly served lunch to me and my partner at our favorite barbecue joint—it was so early on in the fight we weren't picking up on the clues all around us:

The kid's name was Ayric, and he worked at Ready Ribs for my friend who owned the restaurant. From what I knew and observed, Ayric was a standout employee who Robin hoped would someday take over the place. Robin had lost a son of his own, and so he treated this young man as a member of his family. None of us knew Ayric was involved in gang activity until the Westside Rollin' Twenties Blood got shot by a Crip one night after work. I went to visit him in the hospital; I got to hear his story, which kind of kick-started my gangland orientation.

I learned kids who were attracted to gangs didn't necessarily choose that life because they wanted to hurt people, deal drugs, or rip folks off. For boys like Ayric, who had lost his mother from a heroin overdose when he was thirteen, they joined gangs because they wanted to feel accepted, included, and protected. And while we as law enforcement acknowledged the fact gangs would fight over turf, drugs, or money, we were surprised these kids were resorting to using guns to settle personal scores—petty stuff, like wearing the wrong color, or feeling disrespected, or maybe for eyeballing someone's girlfriend.

People in Portland were clueless about how to deal with this new gang phenomenon. It wasn't adults killing each other—it was kids, schoolboys in their teens involved in drive-by shootings, knife fights, and executions over drug deals. It wasn't some Klan white dude killing blacks. It was our little kids shooting each other. We weren't prepared for that. How do you even begin to deal with something so evil? You certainly don't ignore it, which is what everyone outside the police force seemed to be doing—even the church where I worshiped!

One Sunday before the service, a couple of young women who had parked up the street complained that some young thugs from the corner apartments were harassing them. When I overheard their complaints, I walked out of church and up the street to confront the little gangsters. Later, I attempted to rally some of the men to protect the women by standing guard at the corner Sunday mornings to ensure they weren't bothered.

"Hey, let's go out there and explain to these young men you don't treat ladies like that," I implored. But after I heard their response—"Good idea, but that's your job!"—I thought to myself, what a bunch of cowards.

A few weeks later, one of the black kids who had been menacing the girls was shot and killed right up the street from the church. I was so upset I let the clergy have it: "So, you guys believe in this Jesus who protects you and all—unless you actually have to do something! That kid was one of those boys God had put on my heart that we should have been talking to, and you didn't want to do it. You are supposed to be the ones who witness and save young peoples' souls. You had a chance to go up there and minister to these kids, and now one of them is dead. If you don't have anything to say to them, then you don't have anything worth saying. I mean, if you can't address life and death issues in your own community—with your own kids getting killed on the streets—then what are you in church talking about?"

All these people representing themselves as believing in God—it was really only when it was convenient for them. Now remember, I'm going to church in the community, and for years I've been policing those neighborhoods. I've been dealing with all these church people, and then on the street I'm seeing everybody as they are. I'm getting the underbelly of all this stuff—like seeing ministers and pastors up preaching the gospel on Sunday morning, and then seeing them drinking and stealing in their other life. Or seeing these same dudes when they're at home fighting with their wives or getting picked up for DUIs. So I had a pretty good idea of what was really going on with people, and I'm seeing a contradiction here. I'm seeing something ain't right.

I was so frustrated with my church's indifference to the shootings and killings I thought about quitting. But I just couldn't give up bringing attention to what was happening to our kids. I just changed my tactics. I became belligerent and antagonistic towards them. I no longer cared what other people thought of me. I didn't care about protocol. I didn't care about being politically correct.

Needless to say, I wasn't making a lot of friends. It was hard for people to deal with my bad attitude because, as a police officer, I had the authority... and I used it liberally. I was dealing with crazy stuff every day, so then I wanted them to have to deal with crazy stuff. Pretty soon, everybody was asking, "What's wrong with Anderson?"

CHAPTER EIGHT

Dirty, Filthy, Rotten

My partner and I opened the offices of Birkland & Koch in a little rental house down the road from Alpenrose and we outfitted it with one of Grandma's old desks, some chairs, a typewriter, and a couch. My window looked out at a Safeway sign across the street, a view I coveted, especially in the hot summer months. That's because I had an "eighty-five-degree" rule—whenever the temperature read-out hit eighty-five degrees, I would beat the heat by going water skiing or playing golf.

It wasn't that uncommon for prosecuting attorneys like me and Dale to take advantage of our institutional trial experience, switch sides, and begin defending clients charged with criminal offenses. What's rare was being successful at it. What's rare was winning. And that's what we did. But it wasn't easy. Cops—and especially investigators—resented "turn-coats" because they felt betrayed. Everything lawyers like me learned about the inner workings of the criminal justice system would be used against the prosecutors in trial, they rationalized. And they were right.

Five months after I had convicted Ozzie Batchelor of murder when I was still with the DA's office, I won my very first criminal defense case. I earned a not-guilty verdict for my client who was accused of raping

The golf course was where you could find me on a late summer afternoon.

and strangling a high-school girl. I proved the police got the wrong guy. In another, I bested two of my former cop buddies by getting the judge to suppress a confession the detectives got out of my client. I beat them straight up! And my client was guilty!! You want to pick something that really angers the police and the DA's office, it's getting their confession suppressed and losing a case they should have won.

I was well-liked by my peers when I worked in the district attorney's office, but friends became foes as I began to routinely beat them up in the courtroom. Of my first twenty-five murder defenses, only three clients were convicted of murder. And eleven facing murder charges served no prison time at all. As I notched victory after victory over my former allies, the animosity grew exponentially over at police headquarters, and an even wider gap developed in the DA's office. The media didn't necessarily help as they fanned the flames of discord by highlighting my wins and touting my so-called charismatic courtroom antics. I thought it was kind of funny that one reporter compared my emotionally pitched presentations to feverish sermons delivered by a fire-and-brimstone preacher. A full-page spread in the Sunday Oregonian chronicled my success representing rapists, robbers, and murderers under the headline, "Fiery lawyer earns respect in courtroom." One of my former prosecutor pals implied in the article I would stoop to cheating if I thought it would get my client off. But the same guy was also quoted as saying, "If I was charged with murder, I wouldn't mind having him represent me." Another one gave me kind of a backhanded compliment when he said, "He teaches us to be better prosecutors because we know we can't take him lightly."

Their begrudging respect probably bolstered my reputation as a hard-working criminal defense attorney. I think clients were attracted because I had a winning track record. And I got along great with the parents of most of those clients because I truly cared. I would often pray with my clients before trial and was recognized as a man of faith, a Christian in a profession not known for its large contingent of Jesus followers. I was a God-fearing Sunday school teacher whose job happened to be defending men accused of raping teenaged girls and killing young children, women, and elderly men. It was a dichotomy pointed out countless times over my career. When asked how I came to terms with what others saw as an odd contradiction, I would tell them I believe Jesus Christ died for the sins of all men. And if Christ died for them—*all of them*—shouldn't I try to help them?

One of my clients who helped me understand that concept had a Bible verse tattooed on his arm: "Jesus, remember me when you come into your kingdom." It was attributed to the thief on the cross, to whom Jesus replied, "Truly, I tell you, today you will be with me in paradise." Now, the thing is, the thief didn't recite the Four Spiritual Laws; he didn't confess all his sins, he just asked Jesus to remember him. I believe

C8 2M ▇ THE SUNDAY OREGONIAN, JUNE 26, 1983

Fiery lawyer earns respect in courtroom

Birkland sees doing justice as final goal

By JIM HILL
of The Oregonian staff

Some observers liken him to Elmer Gantry.

The flip comparison between criminal defense lawyer Wendell Birkland and the fictional fire-and-brimstone preacher springs from Birkland's fiery, emotionally pitched presentations to juries.

In defense of clients accused of rape, robbery and murder, Birkland might first beg the jurors to show compassion and then demand loudly that they do the right thing: acquit his client.

He gestures profusely and sometimes sights along his outstretched arm and index finger to rivet his piercing blue eyes on one juror or another.

Some observers say Birkland is "gifted," some suggest he might be more style than substance, and one prosecutor said he believed Birkland might try to bend the rules to get a client off the hook. ("I probably feel the same way about some prosecutors," Birkland replied.)

But that same prosecutor, who was the most critical among those asked about Birkland, added, "If I was charged with murder, I wouldn't mind having him represent me."

There is no doubt that Birkland, 36, a former prosecutor himself, gets good results for a lawyer in his line of work. Now working on his 25th murder defense, he says only three of his clients have been convicted of murder. Including three defendants placed on probation, 11 of his murder clients served no prison time at all.

Two of the 25 clients were acquitted, two were found innocent by reason of insanity, four cases were dismissed, and the other defendants either pleaded guilty or were convicted of less-serious forms of homicide.

Birkland has represented people accused of killing small children, teen-aged girls and elderly men and women. One such client was William Perry Jackson, whom Birkland represented in three of the five slayings for which Jackson, 28, is serving life prison terms.

Birkland acknowledges that people sometimes identify him too closely with his clients. He said that after a particularly unpleasant rape case a woman telephoned him and asked, "Do you hate women?"

But if Birkland feels any stigma, he does not show it.

"Most of the individuals I've represented I like," he said, pointing out that most have minimal criminal records and "aren't the horrible people some people think. Nearly always, there's something good to say about somebody."

On the assumption that at least some of his clients are guilty as charged, however, people occasionally ask Birkland how he manages to sleep at night.

Birkland, who is active in the Foursquare Church, said church members have asked the same sort of question.

'Most of the individuals I've represented I like'

"I'm a Christian," he answers. "A person who believes in Jesus Christ believes that Christ died for the sins of all men. If Christ died for them, shouldn't I help them?"

Birkland said people usually do not challenge his explanation.

He acknowledges that "winning" a

WENDELL BIRKLAND

Staff photo by TIM JEWETT

sited his client in jail the man said, "'Mr. Birkland, I didn't do this.' Everything I found pointed to his innocence." The defendant used an alibi defense, and, although there was dispute at trial about the timing, he was acquitted in March 1977 of murder and first-degree rape. The man still lives and works in the Portland area, Birkland said.

"When you see a case like this, you're fighting for justice the same as when you're a prosecutor," he said. Is he still convinced of the man's innocence? "Yeah, I am."

Barry Sheldahl, who for a time was in the same trial unit with Birkland in the district attorney's office, said that case taught prosecutors not to underestimate Birkland. Sheldahl, now an assistant U.S. attorney in Portland, added,

'...That's what I do. I defend people accused of crimes'

"He teaches us to be better prosecutors because we know we can't take him lightly."

In spring 1979, Birkland defended Ralph Milton Jarvis, who was charged with murder in the meat-cleaver slaying of Blanchet House shelter-home manager Vern Tovrea.

The jury found Jarvis innocent by reason of mental disease or defect after hearing the testimony of several psychiatrists, including one who said of Jarvis, "If there is madness, this man has it."

Birkland described Jarvis, who still is in the Oregon State Hospital, as probably the first "truly insane" man he ever had met.

Multiple slayer Jackson, represented by Birkland, pleaded guilty in the slaying of 14-year-old Charmel Ulrich of Sherwood, was convicted by a jury in the killing of Julia Armstrong, 59, in her Sellwood home, and was found guilty by a judge in the death of Calvin Toran, 45, of Portland.

Birkland said that even though Jackson had made statements to police implicating himself in the killings, "I took the cases because that's what I do. I defend people accused of crimes."

He said that despite the brutal nature of the killings, he liked Jackson. Birkland's wife, Kristi, who was the 1971 Rose Festival queen, went to the jail and cut Jackson's hair before he

work. "I'd like to be the best criminal lawyer I can be," he said.

Birkland said his wife and two young children are "extremely understanding" when has to work 12 hours a day, seven days a week preparing for trial. He says he spends considerable time in church activities and only sporadically finds time to golf, ski or water ski.

Birkland, who has driven a Porsche since his college days, admits having been cited for speeding in recent years, and says that as a youth in California he had "a real bad traffic record" that once landed him in jail for five days for speeding.

The experience was "a real eye opener," said Birkland, adding, "I know what it means to want to get out."

> I enjoyed the battle in the courtroom…and the media attention wasn't bad for business. [Reprinted with permission from *The Oregonian*]

he had a full understanding of who Jesus was. And I believe he is in heaven with Jesus today.

While I'll admit there have been some unsavory characters along the way, I actually liked most of the individuals I represented. But there were some observers who felt I went overboard in trying to too closely identify with my clients. And that bothered me. Like the woman who telephoned after I had defended a guy in a brutal rape case. The caller accused me of hating women. But I have remained steadfast in my faith in the criminal justice system. It's the judge and jury who ultimately decide on the crime committed. But if the defense doesn't defend, then innocent people go to jail.

But the people who seemed to have the biggest problem with my vocation were members of my own church. I remember this one high-ranking church lady who demanded to know how I could, in good conscience, represent "dirty, filthy, rotten rapists and murderers." Another, who had heard one of my clients share his redemption story in the adult Sunday school class I taught, scolded me for bringing in a speaker who was "so difficult for some of us to relate to because there are those of us who have never truly entered into sin." That super religious fellow didn't come back to my class again after I reminded him of Romans 3:23, which says, "For all have sinned, and come short of the glory of God."

Somehow, forgiveness for the most horrible just doesn't compute to the average Christian. The mindset of the religious person is, "He's not like us. We just can't relate to people like them." So they don't. They cast them out. They judge. They turn away.

Of course, not all of my clients were easy to love, especially those who committed terribly brutal crimes and then publicly confessed their heinous acts in gory detail. Media reports further publicized the most gruesome cases, helping to make the perpetrators easy to hate. One for whom I took tremendous heat was a white man who was accused of killing five people. I represented him in three of the five murder cases: a fourteen-year-old girl, a fifty-nine-year-old woman, and a forty-five-year-old man. When I got pressed once again by members of my church and others who believed forgiveness was not designed for such a man, I would sometimes answer with the words from a popular children's song:

Jesus loves me! This I know,
For the Bible tells me so.
Little ones to him belong;
They are weak, but he is strong.

Or, I just might break out into song with another relevant kid's Bible chorus:

Jesus loves the little children,
All the children of the world;
Red, brown, yellow,
Black and white,
They are precious in his sight.
Jesus loves the little children
Of the world.

We have this idea that, "Sure, I know Jesus loves me, and I believe Jesus loves all the children of the world, but he certainly doesn't love the dirty, filthy, rotten criminals." But the man I represented in those three murder cases was repentant, he was accepting of his responsibility. I've been with him, I've prayed with him, and I believe God has forgiven him.

I lost each of those three murder defenses and my client was sentenced to life in prison. But over the course of those trials, I came to know him as a human being, not just a murderer. Like Sister Helen Prejean who was Matthew Poncelet's spiritual advisor in the movie *Dead*

Man Walking, I related to my clients not as dirty, filthy, rotten rapist murderers, but as God's children. The guy in the movie wasn't wrongly convicted. He was rightly convicted—a rapist and murderer! Okay, that's who he is. But after he acknowledged his guilt, Sister Prejean says, "You are a son of God, Matthew." And you go, "What?! Dirty, filthy, rotten, rapist murderer—no way is he God's child!" But, to me, that encapsulates best how God sees us. He doesn't see our sin; he sees who we are. God didn't see a thief and a drug dealer and a manipulator and a liar when he saw me. He knew me as his child. That's who he saw.

Most people would reject or fear the men I've represented. But early in my career as a criminal defense attorney, it was my relationship with my clients that shaped my perspective to see people as God sees them— human beings worthy of salvation.

❖

Business was good for Birkland & Koch our first couple years, so we decided to relocate downtown where all the action was. We left the suburbs behind and moved into one of Portland's fanciest high-rises, a strategic move considering the courthouse was right across the street. From my eighth-floor office in the Orbanco Building I could peer directly into the seventh-floor jail. We never did do any advertising to promote our firm, but I jokingly toyed with the idea of trolling for business by putting a neon sign in my window within easy sight of prospective clients: BUSTED? Wanna get out? Call Birkland & Koch!

At the time we had as many clients as we could handle, and I loved it! I think one of the reasons I stayed so busy was due to the fact I could easily relate to law breakers because, well, I had been one. I don't have the record to prove it, but that's only because God spared me that. I couldn't have become a lawyer if I had been busted for the felonies I committed. And it's kind of ironic—that history of lawlessness, plus my conversion and revelation of the living God, prepared me for a career in criminal defense, both spiritually and psychologically.

My prayer was that the people I came into contact with—whether in the courtroom, the jail house, or the Sunday school classroom—would receive God's forgiveness and experience his unconditional love, a love that would lead them down a different path. I did struggle with the notion of evangelism because, as good an orator as I was, I knew I couldn't talk someone into believing in God. But that didn't stop me from sharing my testimony about how God had transformed my life. Proselytizing before a judge and jury in a courtroom was a no-no, so I did the next best thing—I invited clients and their families to meet with me on Sundays. Some weeks there would be more than fifteen clients and/or family members among the seventy-five or so who attended my adult Sunday school class. Many of the righteous "regulars" at Portland Foursquare Church had a hard time relating to the riff-raff, and they constantly let me know how different "those people" were. I sometimes took offense at their holier-than-thou attitudes by verbally sparring with some of the devout over their prejudices. I continued to butt heads with those pious parishioners, but that didn't stop me from bringing the accused criminals I represented to Sunday school. And, as my clientele continued to grow with the addition of a third partner to the firm, more offenders seeking salvation showed up at our place of worship.

CHAPTER NINE

Crazy, Man

People had been calling me crazy for years. When I was bullied as a little boy, I tried to protect myself by putting on an act: I would talk trash; do goofy, silly things to distract my assailants. At school they poked fun at me—calling me "Crazy Legs Anderson"—because my feet stuck out at odd angles, which contributed to my uniquely weird running style. As I got bigger and stronger, my over-the-top intensity on the baseball field and basketball court left many opponents wondering if I had taken one too many hits to the head. And a black cop joining a nearly all-white police force to patrol his own African-American community? Even my friends thought I was nuts.

All I can say is it's a good thing God answered my mom's prayer for me. It was a simple request, one she prayed nightly: "God, don't let my boy die tonight."

I was a knucklehead, out doing everything under the sun that's crazy—all to cover up the fact I was trying to be something I really wasn't—because, quite frankly, I was a scared little kid, basically a coward. But my mom prayed and God has been faithful.

And I was thankful God answered my prayer, too. For a wife. I was almost thirty, and most of my friends were married. And ever since God had prompted me to stop drinking, I wasn't having any fun going out and interacting with a bunch of inebriated people. So I had quit the bar-hopping scene altogether.

God had basically ruined my social life. But apparently, continuing to play the field was not his design for this long-time bachelor. He had the perfect match in mind for me—a strong-minded, independent thinker who, when she first met me, thought I was crazy.

Her name was Renee Wilkerson, an educator from San Francisco who came to Portland for a one-year consulting project. I know she was expecting to return home to her friends and family when the job was done—she had even made a girlfriend in Portland promise not to try to set her up on any blind dates—but me and God had other plans. At a Labor Day party I got invited to, the girlfriend reneged and introduced me. When I took Renee's hand I pronounced, "You're going to be my wife." I wasn't even put off when she told her matchmaking friend she wasn't interested in "that crazy man."

Yeah, you could say I was crazy about her. Me and my buddies—brothers Donald and David Dixon—crashed a party she was at the next Saturday. Renee was cordial as she walked past us, but when she passed by I'm sure she heard Donald tell me, "I thought you told me she was your woman." She was still within hearing distance when I said, "Yeah, but she just doesn't know it yet." Eighteen months later we were married.

Even though she thought I was crazy, Renee Wilkerson became my wife.

Throughout our courtship, marriage, and birth of our first child, I rarely rested. My fellow officers were extremely busy, too. In fact, the year after our daughter, Kenya, was born, there were sixty-three killings, the second most in Portland's history at the time. It got so bad I had to move my family a few miles away from where we lived because gang members were stalking us. They would cruise the alley behind our house, honking their horn as if to say, "We know where you live, Officer Anderson." It was a scary time to be a citizen—or a cop—for that matter.

There were shootings daily—in the morning, nighttime, at schools, at house parties, down the street, at the park. And then there were the calls for service and for shots fired that saturated my district, which was the most active for gang violence. I was tired. I was running from call to call to call.

And even though I often felt like the Lone Ranger without support from the religious institutions, schools, and community groups in the neighborhoods I served, I thrived in my profession. Dangerous? Yes. But I actually enjoyed getting involved in desperate situations, places where I wasn't sure of the outcome.

The only thing that made me walk out there, in the midst of all that uncertainty, was, in a weird way, I liked that stuff. It sounds crazy, but for me, it's the idea of being competitive, of engaging in an activity where you don't know how it's going to turn out. I think that's why I was attracted to police work. Police work is dangerous. It's scary, and that's tough for a coward who had always acted crazy to suddenly be given a gun and authority. I can only imagine the reaction in my community: "You gave that fool—that crazy fool—a gun? And you're letting him loose in my neighborhood?"

As much as I enjoyed the work, there were certain aspects of the job I hated. I was ten years into a twenty-eight-year career with the Portland Police Bureau, and, as a member of an almost all-white police force, I had to deal daily with the pain of alienation from my own black community. But I always felt more hostility from my own organization than I ever did from people on the street.

Seeing some of the white cops respond with disrespect to members of my community caused me to begin to really despise white people in general. That, as well as my personal interactions with them over time, brought me to a place where I had this real animosity in my heart towards white people.

But it was the antagonism I endured when I was out of uniform that bugged me the most. Like the time I was outside the Lloyd Center waiting for a bus to take me to court to testify. A security guard I knew came out laughing, telling me I had just been identified by someone in the mall as the black guy who had stolen her purse. And then there was the racial profiling incident where a white cop pulled me over for no reason. Embarrassed, the policeman let me go after realizing the two of us had worked together years earlier.

But what really pushed me over the edge were the circumstances that caused a state trooper to pick me out of a crowd for a shakedown. I was on my way home from a hunting trip on Mt. Hood when an Oregon State policeman passed by in the opposite direction. After we made eye contact, the trooper made a quick U-turn and singled me out from the procession of hunters' vehicles. He demanded to know whose truck it was and who owned the all-terrain vehicle in the bed, as if a black guy headed down the Mt. Hood Highway with a rifle in the rack and an ATV in the back must be doing something illegal. The patrolman dismissed me without explaining why he pulled me over.

Even though it wasn't proper protocol, I didn't shy away from expressing my opinion about racial profiling and racism on the force. When I got interviewed for a newspaper article titled "Cop vs. Cop," which explored the polarization of the Portland Police Bureau, I was adamant racial profiling existed in Portland: "Absolutely! It's hard for a white person to know what it's like—always being followed, always being watched, always being suspected. And the thing that really added insult to injury was when I shared these experiences, they weren't acknowledged—they were dismissed as isolated incidents."

A white cop quoted in the same article said, "I don't think any of the people I work with are racist," adding that it generally plays out on the street as, "Selling crack cocaine is associated with blacks; selling heroin is generally associated with Mexicans; selling methamphetamine is associated with biker gangs, white people."

Our two cultures were definitely at odds. I admit my enmity toward my fellow white cops—which was seeping over into my feelings for white people in general—was a holdover from my youth and upbringing. There were lots of reasons: hearing white people had no soul, being called a nigger, discovering a history about blacks I didn't read in any textbooks. But the most blatant was the disrespect I felt personally and for the members of my African-American community.

I always felt I had to defend myself within the organization, and at the same time stand up for what's right in my community. I felt trapped between a rock and a hard place. Administration was always talking about how we were all family, how we were all on the same team, but that didn't apply to me. I have never felt the police bureau was my family.

I ultimately worked for the Portland Police Bureau for twenty-eight years.

I was frustrated. And I needed a change of scenery, some type of diversion to protect my sanity. I enjoyed mentoring kids and I loved playing basketball, so I went in search of some extracurricular activities that would satisfy those desires. I corralled my friends, Greg Taylor and Leonard Lamberth, and convinced them we needed to do something positive for the boys in our neighborhood. We decided the best course of action would be to take them out of the city where they could be young men having fun instead of boys dodging bullets.

The three of us committed to walk with this group of young boys over a period of time to see what our impact would be on them. We wanted to create a safe haven for them, hopefully keep them out of the reach of gang influences. Along the way, our intent was to inspire them to dream, to put them in relationship with men who they could talk with about real issues.

We coined it Knucklehead Adventures, probably because I considered myself the original knucklehead. The three of us pooled our own money, drove our own vehicles, and chaperoned the boys on hiking trips to Mt. Hood, rafting down the Deschutes River, and explorations of the Oregon coast. We also instilled principles: Be a person of character. Don't let people of influence or power make you think you're low and they're high. Live your life out by faith. And then a promise: We told them we would keep them together. We promised never to walk away from them.

And the fruit from Knucklehead Adventures is evident today, some three decades later. The guys are grown men now—professionals, husbands, and fathers. Freddie and Eric are police officers, Jesse and Preston in construction. Quick works for a bottling company and Kwain is on Wall Street. But we did lose one boy on the way, gunned down in a phone booth.

Knucklehead Adventures fulfilled a personal ambition in my life—to give back to the community I grew up in and protect some of the fatherless young men closest to me. Work provided another avenue for me to work with youth and serve as a role model when I got the seasonal job of basketball coordinator for the Police Activities League, also known as PAL. The goal of the program was to encourage "at-risk" young people to participate in organized sports-related activities as an alternative to getting involved in gangs. I was excited about this new opportunity and poured myself into organizing events, recruiting volunteers, and preparing for the first-ever PAL Summer Sports Camp where I would be taking the lead on basketball operations. Just like Knucklehead Adventures, this was something rewarding for me that went beyond basic police work enforcing laws and keeping the peace.

But everything got sidetracked when my chief "volunteered" me to hand-hold a member of the Portland Trail Blazers basketball team who had gotten into trouble for punching a female cop during a brawl. The Blazers were in the NBA playoffs and they desperately needed their rookie forward, Clifford Robinson, on the court and not sitting in a jail cell somewhere. So they hooked Robinson up with some fancy criminal defense attorney whose job was to keep cats like him out of the legal system. Now, one might assume getting arrested for assaulting three people—including a police officer—during a fight outside a Portland bar might put most regular people behind bars. But this celebrity lawyer—some guy named Wendell Birkland—got most of the charges dropped and negotiated with the judge for a year's probation and fifty hours of community service. You'd think fifty hours of hard labor picking up litter along Oregon's highways might be in order. Or maybe scrubbing dishes at a homeless shelter. No, Birkland and his friend, the judge, conjured up something cushy—Robinson would serve his time on the basketball court with a bunch of teenagers who were participating in a summer basketball camp. My PAL summer camp!

Bullshit! It was all just a bunch of bullshit. Here I am, a police officer working crime, and now they were telling me they needed me to babysit Cliff. I was like, "I don't think so. I don't need an adult out here who acts like a child. I got to focus on the kids and I got no time to be babysitting your grown ass." But I was essentially told to shut up and just do it. So under protest I went to that first meeting in the attorney's office in one of downtown Portland's high-rise towers, my irritability factor ratcheting up to about a ten as I stepped out of the elevator at the eighth floor. I should have been out patrolling the streets of my Northeast community and putting criminals in jail where they belonged. But no, here I was about to confront the city's best criminal defense attorney—the man whose job was to defend those charged with major crimes like murder, rape, and other hard-core felonies.

I had barely sat down at the table with Robinson and his attorney when Birkland kicked off the meeting with some crude remark like, "Now, Officer Anderson, here's what the judge's order says and this is what you're going to do." I about hit the roof.

At that moment I'm not even thinking about Cliff's stupid ass. I'm focused on Wendell. I don't even see Cliff. Here's this smug white dude sitting up there talking crap, like, "Let me explain to you, officer, how this is going to work…" This is what I hate about the attitude of white people like him—he thinks he's got all the answers. He thinks white people run the whole world. He don't have no idea what's going on.

I don't remember much else about that meeting; it lasted maybe ten, fifteen minutes. But I knew right away I despised that condescending attorney. For him, I could tell it was all business—just another big paycheck. But to me, it was personal. It was about life and history and pain.

There wasn't a lot I could do about it—or to him at the time—but that didn't mean I couldn't entertain thoughts of cruel and unusual punishment for this arrogant attorney. He had the kind of attitude I hate so much I wouldn't say nothing to him if he was on fire. You don't talk to me like that; nobody talks to me like that. You don't even know who I am! What do you mean you're going to dictate to me how this is going to work? Maybe you think I'm some kind of rookie who doesn't understand how this game works.

I couldn't wait to get out of there. And it wasn't until later I learned Wendell had once worked on my side of the law. He was a turncoat, but that didn't make me like him any less. That wouldn't have been possible. I remember thinking as soon as I get out of this office, I won't ever have to see this dude again in my life.

On the way out, Clifford asked me when he should report to my basketball camp to start his probationary purgatory playing hoops with my kids. When we got to the marble floor in the lobby, I let him have it:

"Cliff, let me help you understand how this is going to work. In spite of what your boy in there told you, this is what we're going to do: How about you just not show up at all and we'll just say you did? Does that work for you?"

Now Clifford thought that was quite the deal—fifty hours of community service gone in the snap of a policeman's fingers. Except when the court called to follow up because Cliff didn't show up at my PAL basketball camp. My report was concise and to the point: "He didn't show up. Don't know where he is."

Not my problem anymore, I remember thinking. Not Cliff and not Wendell—I didn't want anything to do with either of them. Oh, I might catch a Blazer game and see the ballplayer on TV, but I was sure I would never see that white attorney again. Because Wendell at that time represented everything I had learned to despise about white people. Everything negative about where I lived and who I was was represented by that stuck-up white dude sitting in that big chair behind his big ol' desk. Our worlds were so completely opposite. Wendell had the country club membership, gated community in the swanky West Hills, Class A office digs, socializing with Portland's upper crust. I couldn't relate. I lived and worked in the same tough Northeast community where I grew up. My friends were the same black kids I played basketball with on cement courts in city parks. I worked for the city, a minority in a nearly all-white police force. My beat patrolling the streets in one of the most dangerous gang-infested neighborhoods in all of Portland put my life in danger every day.

No, the cultural divide between me and Wendell dictated we would never cross paths again. He had tried to dismiss me, but I vowed that day I would forevermore be a foe to what he represented…and I could not be dismissed. So I took on an attitude of opposition. And I perfected my craft. I used my size, my position, my competitive nature, and the fact most people just saw me as a loudmouth ignorant nigger. But they underestimated me.

And I used that to my advantage, too. And this is what Wendell didn't know was sitting in his office.

Little did I know, either, that God had other plans. Because we did meet again. Years later. And our impossible reunion would be even more volatile than our brief encounter with that troubled Trail Blazer. This time it would be personal.

PART TWO

SEPARATED

CHAPTER TEN

My Self-Righteous World

By adding Stephen Houze, formerly a tough competitor, Birkland, Koch & Houze became the dominant player in our niche of criminal defense for more than a decade. We were the proverbial big fish in a small pond, attracting Portland's highest-profile cases in our areas of emphasis: homicide, sexual offenses, drugs, and white-collar crime. Accused murderers, rapists, and drug dealers from all walks of life wanted representation by Birkland, Koch & Houze. And so did many of society's upper crust. There was the long-established Portland jeweler accused of first-degree theft in connection with several armed robberies in wealthy neighborhoods. A county judge who was accused of assaulting his estranged wife. A county commissioner who was charged with official misconduct over allegations he misused county funds.

But the most notorious client had to be Ma Anand Sheela, the chief deputy of controversial Indian guru Bhagwan Shree Rajneesh, who had established a commune in Eastern Oregon. Oregonians were well aware of the shenanigans orchestrated by the two at their free-love community called Rajneeshpuram. Sheela had been charged with attempted murder for plotting to kill the guru's physician in a poison-syringe attack. She was also facing charges for the poisoning of hundreds of people by adding salmonella bacteria to food at area restaurants in an attempt to sicken voters in a county election. And there were additional charges for giving poisoned water to county officials and trying to burn down a county building.

Sheela retained our firm, and I was chosen to represent her in court. The challenge for me was I was right in the middle of jury selection for another murder trial. No one knew when my new client, Sheela, would be extradited from Germany to Oregon to be arraigned on the charges against her. So I proceeded with the jury selection phase. For two days, I had instructed potential jurors that the trial could last several weeks, and I harped on my belief that this case would be the most important one any of them would ever decide in their entire life.

After the second of three scheduled days interviewing candidates, I learned Sheela was back in Oregon. And she was to be arraigned the next morning! To make the arraignment, I would have to ask the judge to delay the jury selection process. Of course, I knew full well there would be media galore at the notorious Ma Anand Shee-la's arraignment. That meant there would be lots of photographs taken of me standing next to my high-profile client. The two of us together would make the evening news. And the next day it would be all over the morning news. And in all the newspapers. Good for business. Great publicity. But what about the dozens of potential jurors with whom I had belabored the point that this murder trial was the most important thing in their lives? What would they think?

I knew—from a career point of view, from a professional perspective—the decision should be to go down there and stand next to Sheela at the arraignment the next morning. But I couldn't do that. All the jurors would have seen the news reports of me being arraigned with Ma Anand Sheela—the most hated woman in the state of Oregon—and here I had told them theirs was the most important case in the world. What a liar I would have been!

So I made the decision that felt right for me. I returned to my jury selection duties, and it was my partner, Stephen, who stood next to our infamous client at her arraignment. From a career sense, it was a bad move for me. But from a God sense, it was the only way to go.

My feeling at the time was to live deeply in my role of helping regular people who for whatever reason got caught up in a major crisis in their life. These people needed my professional help. They also deserved my personal attention and concern. And I'm very aware of the fine line between being the professional attorney hired to represent someone and a friend trying to save their soul in the process. I was careful not to cross that line. It might have made others uncomfortable at times if I offered to pray before we went before the judge, but I think I tried to do it for all the right reasons.

While some attorneys view themselves strictly as technicians, I chose to become deeply involved in the lives of my clients. But sometimes, as my wife has reminded me, that investment can lead to the point of physical, emotional, and spiritual exhaustion. Like the trial of my deaf client who was accused of killing his wife, who was also deaf. While I was listening to the accused man's brother give his testimony, I became so overcome with emotion I had to request a recess to compose myself. It kind of hit home when Kristi read to me what she wrote in her journal after that experience:

> It's been a tough week. Wendell was so upset about his case he's lost twelve pounds in the past two weeks. His pants are all too big in the waist. He's already left for the office (Saturday morning) to meet with a man accused of abusing three children.

I loved the work, but it was exhausting at times. Plus, during the time Houze and I were together—Dale Koch had moved to another firm and eventually became a judge—I was getting more involved in several small-group Bible studies and, of course, my Sunday school teaching. And I had also taken on more of a leadership role in a new ministry called Portland Business Luncheons (PBL). These were monthly gatherings where we would bring in speakers who gave their testimony and encouraged people to build relationships around the person of Jesus Christ.

I know Stephen recognized where my passions outside the firm were leading me, so it wasn't a surprise to either of us when we decided to end the partnership. You can't split the money down the middle if you're going to be gone a third of the time. Not fair to your partner. On my own, I could choose to work fewer cases and make less money. But I knew in my heart if I wanted to do those things, I shouldn't be in a partnership.

I actually stayed put after the partnership dissolved, taking the smaller office with no secretary. The plan was to lower my profile, take fewer cases, and free up more time to do what I believed God was leading me to do. The only problem with that was I got busier working on my own. At the pinnacle of my solo practice, I had thirty cases going on at the same time. My motto at the time was "if it moved and hired me, I took it." But it was too much. The time I had planned to make available to do more of God's work instead became more billable hours, which meant more money. I was juggling a load of clients that typically would have been managed by three attorneys. Unfortunately, I dropped the ball a couple of times and got hit with two malpractice suits. I knew I needed to do something drastic, but it was a heady time. The power, prestige, and paychecks were intoxicating. I remember driving down Sixth Avenue in downtown Portland one morning—probably full of myself—and I believe God interrupted my pride and spoke to my heart.

He said, "Is this being a lawyer a big deal to you? Because I can take it all away. It can all vanish." That hit me hard because, of course, it was a big deal to me. Been doing it for nearly twenty years. Yeah, it was a big deal to me. In fact, it was too big a deal. It got to be too important.

After that encounter I took heed and thought more seriously about whom I would represent and why. First of all, I decided to limit the number of cases to no more than ten at a time. And from that point on, I established new criteria for my clientele. I would take on a new client only if I was convinced the person was ready for spiritual change and was somebody I wanted to be with. Those changes helped me refocus my priorities. To the best of my ability, I began to live out the Scripture that says, "He must increase, but I must decrease." I shed certain clients and refused to take on those that didn't rise to the top of my new filtering system. In the process of scaling down my out-of-control workload, I also determined to remove my name from the list of attorneys available for court-appointed representation. But I got tapped one more time before I could get out of it. And it was a doozy!

In what ended up being my last jury trial of a murder case, I was assigned to represent Laverne Pavlinac, a fifty-seven-year-old woman who had confessed to participating in the rape and murder of a young woman. She then implicated her boyfriend in what turned out to be a bizarre attempt to escape an abusive relationship. In another odd twist, she recanted her fake confession, but it was too late—authorities had no other suspects when she went on trial. I lost the case and she was convicted of felony murder. She and the boyfriend were both sentenced to life in prison, but they were exonerated and released four years later when Keith Jesperson, nicknamed the "Happy Face Killer," confessed to the killing. People still call me when they see me interviewed in reruns of the made-for-TV movie that was produced. Especially my attorney friend, Mike Staropoli, who likes to rib me that I failed because Laverne

Pavlinac was innocent and I got her convicted for murder. He likes to remind me I used to be able to get guilty people off, but now I get innocent ones convicted.

As I was in the process of reducing the number of active criminal defense cases I carried, I continued to attract a full house of current and former clients and their support groups to my adult Sunday school sessions. Whether it was out of curiosity or for condemnation, the faithful at Portland Foursquare Church also flocked to my class. More often than I would have liked, I had to argue my case before church leaders to allow my non-member "fringe-of-society" visitors to attend. Apparently, some members of the congregation were complaining about the difficulty they had connecting with the tattooed, sometimes unkempt invitees, whose sins were so egregious compared to their own. They would try to convince me that because they didn't think their sins were as filthy as those of my clients, they were somehow different than them, somehow better than them. I had to remind them that's not what God's word says. Even though my clients might have acted or looked different, God loved them just as much as he loved the long-time members, and we should welcome them at church.

One particular Sunday, when I was still stewing over the reckless discrimination that once again had reared its ugly head in my classroom, God tapped me on the shoulder and rudely reminded me of an earlier time when intolerance ran rampant...and I had done nothing to stop it. It was back when Kristi and I were teaching the junior high Sunday school class. Portland Foursquare had no African-American members, but for a period of time they used to bus kids in from outlying neighborhoods, including a handful of black kids. James Pankie was one, a much quieter boy than "Governor" Lewis—that's what he called himself—who was a rambunctious black boy I later encountered in the criminal justice system. The church ultimately ushered James and

Governor out, along with two rowdy girls who wore rat tail combs in their hair, letting them know they were no longer welcome. The buses soon stopped transporting the black kids, and the church returned to its white-only ways.

I was mad at the racists who kicked those black kids out of the church, but I didn't do anything to reclaim them. I mean, those were my kids, and I didn't do anything to try to protect them. I stayed with my people, the white folks. I said it was wrong, but they got chased out of church, and I just went on teaching Sunday school and trying cases.

Did that make me a racist, too? It certainly was a blind spot, but no one up to that point in my life had ever described me as prejudiced or a bigot, a man who looked down on others because of their skin color or social or economic status. Now, I certainly qualified as having all the benefits of what one might perceive as white privilege—family wealth, expensive education, kids in Christian school, nice home, respected social status, fancy office, cars, etc. And the less obvious advantages ascribed to me as a white male, such as the freedom to live, play, and work wherever I wanted? At the time, I wasn't aware of all the exclusive benefits I enjoyed as a Caucasian man living in an all-white neighborhood and working in a profession dominated by whites. Why? Because I didn't have to. This was Portland, Oregon, after all, widely recognized as the whitest major city in the country. There weren't any black families in my church, I didn't know of any living on the west side of Portland, and I didn't socialize with any African Americans. There was certainly no grand design to avoid interacting with black people. That's just the way it was. Intentionally crossing that line to integrate my life with others of different skin color was simply not on my radar screen.

I thought everything was wonderful. Hey, I'm a believer! I hung out with guys who were following Jesus. I taught Sunday school. No black people there? That's just the way it is, right? What could I do about it?

I got this whole outreach-to-the-lost-in-prison thing figured out. But are we ever going to break down the barriers of racism? Well, shoot, that ain't my job. That's hopeless! To me, in my self-righteous world, everything was fine at the time.

But there was a problem. And its tentacles stretched well beyond the white-washed walls of religious places like Portland Foursquare Church and Portland Business Luncheons. It wasn't that the plight of African Americans and other minorities was ignored by me and Oregon's so-called white Christian leaders—we just never thought about it! Never considered the black condition. Until it showed up on my doorstep in the form of two of the biggest African Americans I had ever encountered. One was young, rich, and in trouble with the law. The other was the law. And it seemed to me he was mad at the entire world.

I was used to representing celebrities, so when I got a call that one of the Portland Trail Blazers needed representation, I took the case. It was pretty straightforward: Blazer rookie Cliff Robinson had been at a club celebrating a playoff win when a fight broke out in the parking lot of Goldie's Restaurant & Lounge. One of the responding officers attempted to break up the brawl, but in the ensuing melee she got hit in the head and knocked to the ground. She identified Robinson as the man who struck her and arrested him on four misdemeanor charges.

It wasn't that big of a case for me; the only reason it was a big deal is it was Cliff Robinson, a Trail Blazer. Gee, when Cliff gets busted he calls me—that's good. Compared to all the murder cases I had tried, this was a lot less serious. This was a little discussion with the DA's office and a paycheck. It was so trivial, I mean really, in the broad scheme of life, this was such a minor thing. Cliff wasn't a bad man; he was just a twenty-one-year-old kid who did something he shouldn't have done.

I ended up getting the charge for assault on a police officer dismissed and Cliff got probation and fifty hours of supervised community service, with a stipulation his work had to be documented by someone at a credible agency, like a non-profit organization. The only other thing I had to do was facilitate a meeting with my client and the police officer—a cop named Larry Anderson—who was assigned the follow-up on Cliff's community service.

I think Cliff got to my office first, and then in walked this huge black cop—probably six-foot-six, 250 pounds—in his police uniform. I had never met him, but I could tell in a second he wasn't happy to be there. I took charge, started reading him the order, and it was kind of funny—I looked over at him and I could tell he hated my guts. But to me that was irrelevant because he had to do what he had to do. I mean, he couldn't hurt me. If he did, he would lose his job, his wife, his family, his house. Does it matter if he's mad, doesn't like me? It doesn't matter.

I could tell as soon as we sat down that Officer Anderson hated my guts.

I had already gotten my result; this was just excess. My interaction with two black men that day didn't mean a whole lot to me, but I could tell something was majorly wrong with the black cop. The bad attitude. The look on his face—full of contempt, and probably hatred. I could sense the ill will, but I was oblivious as to why Officer Anderson felt that way. I had had to deal with the animosity in the police department toward me for crossing the line from prosecutor to defender, so

109

maybe this cop was mad about that. To me it was just a day in the life of a defense attorney. I had no idea what that cop's problem was. I guess I really didn't care much about it...until years later when we met again. And he told me I was the problem.

CHAPTER ELEVEN

Crisis of Faith

Even though I continued to be sort of a lightning rod for controversy—especially during my three-year "time-out" from street cop when I worked a desk job in Personnel as a minority recruiter—I hadn't alienated everybody…yet. But they did transfer me to North Precinct where, fortunately, I got along great with my new partner, John Frater, a black cop with whom I developed a friendship over the years we patrolled together. While I remained guarded in my relations with other members of the police force, I felt comfortable around John, even to the point of giving him religious tracts to read. When you spend eight hours a day in the same car with your partner—putting your life in his hands in one of the most dangerous professions—you figure you would get to know the guy pretty well. The day I found out I didn't really know John Frater at all changed my life. There were actually two days of enlightenment—the day I discovered my partner had a gang-banger for a son, and the day that gang-banger was shot and killed.

John had never mentioned he had a son from his previous marriage, a fact that puzzled me because I assumed friends would share those types of intimate details. I only found out in the course of duty when John and I responded to a call about some African-American kids acting suspicious.

When we arrived, we saw two young black men sitting in a car with the roof sawed off. As was our routine, I was the more aggressive one and jumped out of the car first, while my more laid-back partner stayed behind.

I get up there and I'm jacking these two young dudes up, and they're being smart asses. When I asked the one kid his name, he says, "John."

"Okay, John, what's your last name?"

"Frater."

"You trying to be funny here? You a smart ass, huh? You're John Frater, huh?"

"Yeah."

"Come on then, let me see your ID, boy." After picking up the wallet the surly kid threw at me, I read the name out loud.

"John Frater. John Frater? John Frater Jr.?" Turning to look back at my partner who had this sheepish look on his face, I asked the boy, "Is that your father?"

"That's my biological father, but he ain't no father to me." WHOP, I slapped him good across his face.

"Don't you be disrespectful! Boy, I don't care what you think of your father, but he's always your father. Now you guys get to steppin' on outta here before you got a problem."

When I turned back to my partner, I'm sure I had this confused look on my face. "John, what's up? Man, he's in a gang. You didn't even tell me you had a son."

When someone close to you chooses not to confide in you, a normal reaction would be hurt feelings, maybe a little anger, some bitterness. But I only felt shame. I was ashamed I didn't know anything about my partner's son. Because if we were truly friends—like I thought we were—then I felt I should have known. Here I am, preaching at him, handing him religious tracts, inviting him to church, and I don't know this? I'm looking at him every day and I can't see the disappointment and hurt inside him? What a shame.

That run-in with my partner's son—a gang member in the neighborhood his dad patrolled—shook my confidence. Was I not a good friend? Did my partner not trust me? As close of friends as I thought we were, shouldn't I have known? These questions pestered my conscience. It didn't really change our relationship, but for the next several weeks I noticed our conversations were more surface-oriented: "How 'bout them Trail Blazers?" "Have you seen that such-and-such movie yet?" "I can't believe all this rain we're having." And hardly any, "How's the family?" "You doing okay?"

But when I really thought hard about my relationship with John, I had to check myself: Did I ever ask about his family? Did I even care if he had a son or not? I struggled to come up with honest answers.

Weeks later, on an August morning, John and I were starting our day shift when we heard a radio report about a shooting. A commander then tracked down John at the precinct and told him officers needed him at the scene. I knew right away what that meant. I looked at my partner. Neither of us needed to say anything. I just knew I had to go with him. I said, "Come on man, let's go." When we arrived, there was a body on the ground, covered. John stayed in the car while I slowly walked over to the lifeless form and pulled back the blanket. It was John Frater Jr.

As I knelt beside the body, I turned to see what the boy's father was doing. Officer John Frater Sr. was still sitting in the car, with a pained look on his face, just staring. Makes me cry every time I think about it. And I'll never forget the chilling conviction I felt when I looked hard at my partner, a parent who had just lost his son: it's like I saw his face for the first time in my life. We were together five years, man, and I ain't never seen his face. When I saw that part of him and realized who that was—a flawed, lost, and hurting human being—it decimated me. When I locked eyes with him, it was like I finally saw the real John Frater...and I saw myself.

At that moment I realized what was wrong. It wasn't them—the black clergy, the church, the community—it was us. We were the problem. I was the problem. Because I'm out here playing, thinking this is some kinda game.

It hit me right then when I was kneeling over my partner's son's dead body—this ain't no game, and they aren't playing.

That's when God changed my life for real. Right then I knew I was a different person. I knew I wasn't going to pretend anymore. I wasn't going to play with people any more. This wasn't a game. This was serious business. At that time in my career, I knew I had compromised myself so I could get along with people, so I could survive. I was talking all this religious crap, talking all over people, but I didn't see them, I didn't see their pain. I wouldn't let myself relate to them.

Up until that moment, I had believed because we were the good guys, bad things shouldn't happen to us. Police officers' sons don't get swept up into gang violence. Neighbors' kids don't die in gang violence. The good guys—the cops—we were supposed to help keep them safe. It was the bad guys who were making all the wrong decisions, so they were the ones who should suffer the consequences of their actions. Right? But that wasn't my reality.

The death of John Frater Jr., and the fact I didn't even know my partner had a son, jump-started some drastic changes in my life. If I was going to stay in this profession and continue policing my own neighborhoods, I couldn't go on as I had. That was the first incident that shook me to the point where I thought, man, I got to do something more. How can I explain my partner's son on the ground, dead? Ain't never coming back again. I mean, we're not protected from this kind of stuff? We're the good guys out here doing the right thing, but we ain't doing enough.

That's when I realized I had just been going through the motions. I didn't take anything personal. Didn't let my emotions get involved. Didn't get attached to people. Didn't associate with them. I was just the police. That all came crashing down when a young punk named John Frater Jr. got killed in a drive-by shooting. It was like God threw down the gauntlet and said, "That's not good enough anymore!"

That's when it got personal. From then on, I realized I had to be emotionally involved. I knew I had to do something more than I had been doing. For me, personally, how I had been living and acting just wasn't acceptable. When I saw my partner's face as he was sitting in that car, I realized I had violated the very thing God says: "Give up your life; lay it down."

One of the lessons I was learning the hard way was I couldn't fix the problem. There was real suffering by people who were no better or worse off than I was. They felt tremendous pain, not because they were bad people or because they did something wrong. They were suffering because that's what happens sometimes in a broken world.

They buried John Edward Frater Jr., age twenty-one. And life went on. So did a whole lot of dying in North/Northeast Portland. After a while, I concluded my environment had become a cloud of death, one my brain couldn't even process. But I wasn't going to give up. Yes, I had to change my way of thinking. No longer would I buy into the myth that because I carried a badge and wore a policeman's uniform, I would be protected from the consequences of terrible things happening on my watch.

That's when everything changed for me. My partner's son dying catapulted me into the emergency of the situation. It changed the way I looked at things; I was no longer a bystander who is a police officer. I was actively, personally involved right in the middle of the mess. Everything I thought was a sanctuary or safe haven—the very neighborhood where I grew up—had evolved into a danger zone. And we had no idea how to protect our young people from killing each other. Sure, the bureau had by then created a Gang Enforcement Team, but they staffed it with all white officers! And they just made things worse by applying their traditional police response, which basically criminalized black culture. To them, every black kid who wore red or blue was a gangster. We called them "cowboys" because they were riding herd on African Americans who lived in Northeast Portland—serving search warrants, kicking in doors, and arresting black people left and right. All in front of Portland's TV news cameras. It was a fiasco! And they were driving the local community into hysteria.

There were a number of us African-American officers who had signed up to be on the gang team, but none of us was selected. We made enough noise, though, that five of us eventually got added to the Gang Enforcement Team—basically by executive order. More than 100 kids had died by then, and I was committed to stemming that tide.

My first task was to get educated about this whole gang phenomenon—a process that taught me so much I ended up taking on the role of Intelligence Officer, specializing in LA-style street gangs. What I learned frightened me. I came to the stark realization we were at the forefront of a dangerous new episode in Portland's history—a cancer so insidious the community-at-large was oblivious to it. Unlike in other larger cities where there were distinct Blood or Crip territories, North/Northeast Portland had few areas of gang concentration. Typically, members of warring gangs lived across the street from each other, went to the same schools, attended the same churches, and played in the same parks. That's what made the work for me so difficult—the kids in my community were always in each other's faces, which made for an extremely volatile and very unpredictable situation.

I felt a huge sense of duty to protect these kids who lived and now were dying in my neighborhood. It was an overwhelming responsibility, so I figured the best approach was to try to educate those in positions of authority. I initially contacted the black pastors and clergy that represented the predominantly African-American population of inner Northeast Portland. First, I needed to make them aware of the mushrooming gang presence, and then solicit their support in trying to educate parents and their kids about the potential dangers of gang involvement. Several meetings and frustrating exchanges later, the pushback began to sound similar: "Gang violence is police business," the church leaders told me.

So I moved on...to more receptive audiences. I took my message about the pending dangers of the growing gang presence to other law enforcement and government agencies, schools, businesses, hospitals, corporations, etc. I was basically a clearinghouse regionally and nationally for what is and what isn't a gang activity: "Johnny was wearing red shoes with red shoe strings; is that a gang?" After several years in the process, I was getting upwards of ten speaking requests a week.

But it was one question from a local county commissioner that stopped me short: "It seems like everything you guys do is after the fact. You have all these resources for after somebody shoots somebody; what are you doing before they get into trouble?"

She was right. We did intervention and response, but nothing related to prevention. When we looked into what other cities were doing to try to prevent kids from joining gangs, we discovered a model called G.R.E.A.T., which stands for Gang Resistance Education and Training. The violence prevention program is school-based and is taught by law enforcement officers in the classroom. It was a perfect match for me and the city of Portland at the time, so I seized the opportunity to intensify my role in the fight against criminal gang activity. I became the bureau's G.R.E.A.T. coordinator, which was a position underwritten by the federal Bureau of Alcohol, Tobacco, Firearms, and Explosives. And I quickly rose in stature to become a spokesperson for the organization, traveling around the region to teach and train others about gang prevention strategies.

But my expertise and regional exposure did not change the fact African-American kids in my neighborhood were continuing to die from gang violence at an alarming rate. I thought I was doing all I could to make a difference. And I also knew that wasn't enough. I needed help.

I thought maybe now with my new status as an official spokesman for gang prevention, the local community might be more receptive to my message. So I tried again to do what had failed before in my own church and with other black clergy. With renewed vigor, I called the leaders of the community together. I met with the black church leadership. I called on pastors. I visited schools to plead with the principals. I petitioned higher-ups in city government. Through G.R.E.A.T. I was empowered with teaching materials and other tools designed to educate and motivate citizens to act. So I made dozens of presentations. Spent nights and weekends of my own time. All in a renewed effort to wake up the community to the reality they needed to be part of the solution in preventing gang activity. The bottom line? If there was a press conference or a funeral, the so-called community leaders would show up. Otherwise there was just a lot of talk and no action.

At that point, I was ready to give up on the church. Telling them about the gang problem wasn't working—because people were saying it really wasn't that bad. So I came up with another idea—some show-and-tell—hoping that would bring them to their senses. I created a display with pictures of guns that police had recently confiscated from neighborhood kids. Then I told them I had a story behind each weapon—all fifty of them. Even though they couldn't refute the facts, they weren't swayed. Desperate to make them understand, I returned later with pictures of all the kids killed by gang-related violence and threw them down in front of the so-called black leadership. They were indifferent, and that had a profound effect on me. My confidence in the church—the institution I grew up in, the place where I began my own faith journey—was wavering. It wasn't so much I began to doubt or criticize God, I just felt the people who were saying they represented God were full of crap.

And now, when I'm confronting them with this problem of our kids getting killed, they don't want anything to do with it? I'm like, "What else are you doing? Is there some other agenda more important than this?"

The church didn't have a satisfactory answer, which meant my strategy to solicit help from the black clergy wasn't working. They just didn't seem to grasp the severity of the problem, even as the frequency of gang shootings increased. That didn't make them bad people; in fact, I knew most of them to be compassionate and kind—they just had no solutions to offer. And that let me down, mightily. I finally had to say, "If God, through you, has nothing to say to them, then I have no use for that kind of religion."

That resignation began what I would call my crisis of faith, although it was a faith misplaced. I used to have faith in the black pastoral leadership, faith in the church, but after their lack of response to the gang violence in their own backyards, I began to realize these people in leadership roles weren't any different than any other kind of exclusive club that only served its members and nobody else. I had been sold on the premise they were the guardians of our people, and therefore I should be placing my trust in them to help out when needed.

At that point I didn't have the answer. The police department didn't have any answers. Obviously, the church and the religious people didn't have any answers. So I thought, "What use are you?"

The war still raged between the Bloods and the Crips. Racism was rampant at the police bureau. And no one in the community seemed willing to step up and help address the problems that had created such a mess. I was hurting and I felt alone. With no other resources to call on, I eventually turned to my Heavenly Father. Actually, I just about turned my back on God was what I did.

Months went by where it seemed there was at least one gang shooting every day. And at least one dead young African American every week. For someone like me, who lived and worked in the community where the fighting and shooting and dying was going on night and day, it was very distressing. Nerves were frayed. Everyone seemed on edge. There was no peace.

After a particularly disturbing night of gunfire and bloodshed—with another young teen lying dead on the street—I reached the end of my rope. I went through the motions of interviewing witnesses, tracking down leads, and filing my report. Exhausted, depressed, confused, I got back in my squad car and just sat there. And then the emotions came bubbling up. I felt abandoned by my community. Betrayed by the clergy. Misunderstood by my fellow officers. I was alone and angry. I felt like screaming. So I did. At God.

"All the killings, God, it has to be a curse from you," I cried out. "That's why we can't protect our children. It's a curse! We don't honor you. So how can we have any expectation you would deliver us from anything? What good is any of our stuff if we can't stop our kids from killing each other? So I'm done believing you're going to do anything! I'm not going to church anymore. I'm not going to pray like I'm religious. I'm done with all that!"

After I told God off, I just sat there. There was no retaliation, no lightning bolt to strike me dead for sassing the Lord. But I did get a response.

"Finally!" I sensed God say. "All that stuff you're doing, I never asked you to do any of it. I'm the one who should carry those burdens. And, as a matter of fact, I didn't even ask you to believe in me. I believe in you. I chose you. You didn't choose me."

Immediately I felt a burden lifted. My soul-searching questions weren't necessarily answered, but I heard what I needed to hear: "Place your burdens in my hands. Trust me."

Over the next few months, I wrestled with letting go…and letting God. There was no miraculous decline in the number of gang-involved shootings. The clergy, the community, my fellow white police officers, they didn't rush to my side and offer any more support than they had before.

I was still angry, still bitter over the fact nothing seemed to change the situation. I did withdraw from the church. I also stepped away from any involvement with the black religious leadership. I basically decided I was not going to try to manufacture anything anymore. So I waited on God. And waited and waited.

With no more revelations coming from above, I figured me and God were kind of at a stalemate. But I still couldn't shake the fear that because of all the iniquities of my people, God had truly abandoned us, and more kids would die. And that infuriated me to no end. I couldn't lash out at my Creator again, but while in this state of mind, woe to anyone who might approach me with their racist or religious bullshit.

That's when the old white dudes showed up.

CHAPTER TWELVE

Everyone Was White!

Maybe I was color blind, if the definition of that practice allows white men like me to not recognize how the non-white population is disadvantaged. And especially in Oregon where there aren't a lot of African Americans. For me and my white friends, it was out of sight, out of mind.

That was made glaringly obvious in the fall of 1992 when a group of us helped orchestrate a Christ-centered outreach called Oregon Vision. The idea was actually a concept championed by another Oregonian— Doug Coe, who lived in Washington, DC, and was the driving force behind the National Prayer Breakfast. The vision for Coe's beloved Oregon was that during a three-day period, he and 400 men and women in groups of three to four would visit every city in the state— with no agenda other than to mention the name of Jesus and offer to pray with and for those in leadership roles.

It was a monumental leap of faith and a logistical challenge, but my attorney friend Victor Anfuso and I and dozens of other volunteers spent months working on an Oregon Vision that forever altered the spiritual landscape of a state recognized as one of the least churched in the union. Mayors, police, pastors, firemen, teachers, laymen, and businessmen and women in 180 cities, towns, and communities enjoyed the blessings of a word of encouragement and a friendly touch. As a result of the visit to every Oregon city with at least a population of 1,000, untold numbers of new small groups of community leaders started meeting weekly around Christ for prayer, accountability, and support.

Afterwards, all of us reconvened at a Central Oregon resort where we shared our experiences and received a challenge from Coe to continue the work we had started. As Vic and I looked around the room, we saw the glow on the faces of the hundreds gathered in celebration. Some 140 of Coe's associates had come from out of state to join in this spiritual quest. The rest of the 260 were locals, representing Oregon's three major regions—Eastern Oregon, Southern Oregon, and the Willamette Valley, which included Portland. Everyone was happy.

"Love is a person by the name of Jesus," Coe shared. "If you're filled with Jesus, you're filled with unconditional love and you can love everybody. Only in Jesus is there no bond nor free, no black nor white, no rich nor poor. Make it your goal to be one in the Spirit and you'll ultimately be at peace with each other."

Amens all around. I caught Vic's gaze. And we nodded in agreement. As I scanned the room again, I saw love. Like the assembled, I was soaking in Coe's words: "Only in Jesus; no bond nor free; no black nor white..." As my head swiveled from left to right, and back again, it struck me. Yes, love was everywhere. Yes, everyone was happy. In fact, everyone looked the same. Everyone was white!

On the four-hour drive back to Portland—later dubbed Whitelandia by a local minority group—Vic and I couldn't shake the thought something had been missing from an otherwise successful Oregon Vision. Hundreds of lives had been impacted for good. Many new relationships developed. Small groups centered on Christ were proliferating. It was all good! Halfway home, as we passed by glorious snow-capped Mt. Hood,

Victor arrived at the realization that would change his perspective. The vision for Oregon—sharing the love of Christ—that he, I, and some 400 believers had just delivered to thousands, was meant for all Oregonians. Whether through oversight or indifference, the reaching out to "all" didn't happen to include people who weren't white. Lesson learned. I was less moved, but Victor determined to do something about it.

A few weeks later when my wife and I were just finishing up dinner, the phone rang. It was my friend, Vic, who was talking frantically about some big meeting going on. "Are you kidding me?" I blurted out after Vic told me he wanted me to join him at this black guy's house, like *right now!*

I had no idea what I was getting myself into—he had only given me a street address—but I figured Vic's call must have had something to do with his revelation from the recent Oregon Vision that us white guys should start reaching out to the blacks. Before I hung up, I told him I would go grudgingly because I had no expectations any of the black men would want to meet with whites. In fact, I told him it was hopeless.

I was quite familiar with the area the directions took me—Laurelhurst was a coveted, well-to-do neighborhood where I think the governor of our state lived. I wondered who this big-shot black guy might be as I knocked on the massive front door. My jaw about dropped to the floor as I recognized the presence filling the front hallway—it was the huge black cop I had encountered three years earlier over the Cliff Robinson case. *It was Officer Anderson, the guy who hated my guts.* And from the look of recognition on his face and the squint of his eyes, I could tell his opinion of me had not changed.

With some trepidation, I sat with Vic and a handful of other white businessmen as the awkward moments played out in the Andersons' living room. There were a number of younger black men—they looked like they could all start for an NFL football team—on the other side of the room, all staring at us as if we needed to make the first move. That's when Victor gave his impassioned plea about how important it would be for blacks and whites to get to know one another, to build relationships, even friendships. But as I watched the assembled black guys grow more and more uncomfortable listening to the presentation, hopeless became impossible in my mind. There seemed to be zero interest on their part.

Anderson finally provided some feedback, but it was more of a rant. He basically said he wanted nothing to do with white people and their religiosity. And then he called me out as his example of what's wrong with white men and their privileges. I'd had enough. On my way out the door I reminded Vic I thought this notion of racial reconciliation was hopeless. I think Officer Anderson overheard me because he said something like, "that's the only time me and Birkland will ever agree on anything."

CHAPTER THIRTEEN

Don't Need You White People!

No, it couldn't be. But there he was—the same arrogant attorney I had vowed never to set eyes on again. And he was at my front door. It had been a couple years, but I reluctantly recognized Wendell Birkland as the slick, aristocratic, skinny white dude who had sanctimoniously ordered me to babysit that Trail Blazer brat, Cliff Robinson.

As rare as it was, I had actually been expecting a couple of white guys to show up at my house that evening. I had just returned home from a dinner attended by a bunch of older white businessmen and my African-American friend, Waverly Davis, who had invited me. The purpose of the gathering, I learned, was to identify leaders of the black community to whom leaders of the white community could reach out in an effort to establish cross-cultural relationships.

The impetus for the local outreach was inspired by an attorney named Vic Anfuso who talked about his recent "white-only" experience at something he called Oregon Vision. But it was also timely in that a nationwide Christian men's movement, Promise Keepers, was promoting a pledge of racial reconciliation. Waverly had recommended to the white businessmen that, because I had intimate knowledge of who Portland's black leaders were, they should seek my counsel. They wanted to know which African-American pastors and community leaders could I introduce them to because, well, they were the leaders, the ones black families in North and Northeast Portland looked up to, right? That had hit a hot button with me, a community servant who had run into a brick wall every time I had approached the clergy and men of the community to help me maintain peace in what had become a gangland territory. "They're not the leaders as far as I'm concerned," I told them. And then I went on to explain why I felt that way. After my tirade, the organizers of the meeting were at a loss how to proceed.

To this day, I have no idea how I got roped into hosting an after-dinner "conversation" about race relations at my house later that night. The white guys apparently didn't want to drop the subject, so they persuaded me to invite over some of my black friends—and they called some more of their associates—to reconvene at the Anderson residence.

When I got home from the dinner at Vic's, I quickly shared with my wife I had met a bunch of old white men who must have been feeling guilty because now they wanted to be friends with black people. What I failed to mention earlier was there were about twenty guys headed to our house.

Renee wasn't the only one who would be upset with me before the night was over. In a pinch, I had just called a dozen of my buddies and told them to show up at my house as soon as possible. I gave no explanation why. They were all my friends, guys who grew up together playing sports. Like me, they were big, black, and athletic. And, just like me, none of them seemed pleased to be part of whatever the white guys had dreamed up.

The tension in my living room hit the boiling point about twenty minutes into Victor's passionate speech as he pontificated about racial reconciliation—how black men and white men should start building relationships, and why they should begin meeting in small groups to talk about

Jesus. I saw my guests begin to shift uncomfortably where they sat, casting sideways glances at each other and steely darts in my direction.

They didn't have to verbalize what they were thinking. They wanted out. And they wanted answers: "What's the deal here, man?" "Why you set us up like this?" Even Renee, who was listening from another room, was peeking her head out and giving me "the look," as if to say, "This is really bizarre, and you should wrap this up soon."

When Vic finished, Waverly attempted to speak on behalf of us black men, suggesting more meetings and the need to continue the conversation. But none of us was nodding in agreement. It became quite awkward—the white men waiting to hear what the black guys thought, and the black men showing no interest in saying a single word. Soon, everyone in the room was looking at me. As a policeman, I was used to taking charge. And as a black man in my community, I had no problem speaking my truth to this group of white men.

"Look," I began, "you see these guys here? These are my friends. This is my house. This is my wife. I got a job. Why do I need to try to be friends with white people? I don't need you white people coming over and trying to fix me, thinking there's something wrong with me. I'm not broken! I got the same kind of shortcomings all humans have, but I got a life here. I got friends; I don't need white people in my life—especially Mr. 'White Privilege' Birkland over here. You don't need to save me; you don't need to show me Jesus. I know Jesus. Why would I need to be in a little group with a bunch of old white men who I don't know and I don't trust?"

The first attempt at a racial reconciliation effort in Portland was over. After the white guys left, my friends immediately demanded an explanation for why I had rousted them from their homes this late at night. And for what? To listen to a bunch of white guys they didn't know telling them stuff about "racial reconciliation" they didn't want to hear?

As they stomped out of my house, I didn't even try to explain. I was embarrassed. I had invited them over as a favor for Waverly, but everything had backfired. And now I felt I had just jeopardized my relationship with some of my closest companions. Before they all abandoned me, I grabbed my two best friends—Greg and Leonard. We had been hanging out together since we were little, and I felt I owed them an explanation.

I hadn't related this to the larger group, but I felt compelled to tell them why I had agreed to have Vic and his crew over. Yes, it had started as a favor for Waverly, but when I had found out at the dinner earlier that evening how misguided Vic and the other so-called white leaders were, I wanted to straighten them out.

Obviously, I must have said something at Vic's dinner meeting about the lack of leadership in the black community that caused everyone to drop what they were doing and race over to my house. I could sense my friends' skepticism, so I assured Greg and Leonard I wasn't saying they were the ones who needed to step up and assume the mantle of black leadership in Portland, Oregon. Or that we would ever have to meet again with those same white guys who had just left with their tails between their legs. But I did want to remind them of something the three of us had experienced:

> You remember that pact we made when we were sixteen, seventeen years old, sitting on the corner of Fifteenth and Prescott? It was maybe two, three in the morning. We had just been walking around, hanging out, probably smoking weed, and somehow we got serious. We were talking about this "Creator" we had been hearing about and we made a promise. We told each other we were always going to obey God. Well, I believe God spoke to me that night. He told me I would go before kings and queens and speak. Now, I know that sounds weird, but I believe God has something very special planned for us!

It was getting late, and we all had lots to think about. Were we willing to invest ourselves deeper into race-related issues facing our community? And,

frankly, I'm sure Greg and Leonard were asking themselves what cou̶
accomplish? One was a city maintenance worker, the other a bus driver. T̶
weren't a cop like me, or lawyers like those white guys—people seemingly̶
on the front lines of dealing with gangs and racism.

As I walked them to my front door, I knew what the three of us were
wondering: would we ever see those white dudes again? "We'll see," I said
quietly. "We'll see."

When I came back to the kitchen for a glass of water after a long and unset-
tling evening, there was Renee, hands on hips and looking serious. I thought
I might get admonished for ruining her night by bringing all these guys over
and causing such a ruckus. I was relieved and mystified by her comment:

"Sweetie, you can be friends with anybody, even old white men."

As I followed her up the stairs, I muttered to nobody in particular, "We'll see."

CHAPTER FOURTEEN

Dekum

Driving home that night—across the river, through the West Hills, and into our gated community—I rationalized my case in my mind. The attorney in me brought up some good points: "Larry Anderson hated me the first time I met him and I got the same feeling from him tonight. We tried, but they made it pretty clear they don't want to meet with us. That's fine, because I really don't want to start some small group meeting with them either—I'm already over-committed." By the time I had parked the car in the garage, I had pretty much convinced myself—for a bunch of good reasons—I would not be participating in any future racial reconciliation efforts.

But by morning my case began to crumble. When Victor initially pointed out we were disregarding African Americans at our Portland Business Luncheons and during Oregon Vision—and that we should be reaching out to them—I responded negatively. That's basically who I am. But then I consulted the Lord and felt convicted I'm to do it. I think God wanted to show me at the time, "You dummy, this isn't about sacrifice, it's about obedience. I told you to do this—just do it and shut up!" So when Victor called to follow up, I agreed to be available should any future meetings with the black guys be scheduled.

In spite of how busy we were and how poorly we all thought that first meeting went, there was talk about setting up a regular Tuesday night gathering. But I was still skeptical. The caveat running through my mind at the time was, "Hey, I'm a good guy. I made the effort. I tried. I reached out with open arms, but it didn't work. If they want to do it again—*if they really want to do it again*—well, I'll show up."

I was still reluctant, still second-guessing my decision to participate in another session about race relations as I drove to that first Tuesday night meeting. Once again, Vic had given me an address, but no other details. I immediately recognized Dekum, the street where a black pastor who would host the meeting lived. I was familiar with the street because it was associated with the first murder case I ever prosecuted. Two men had killed another, tried to burn his body in the furnace of a downtown building, and then attempted to hide the evidence—a gas can and a shovel—in a garbage can on Dekum Street. As I passed that crime scene and pulled up to the pastor's house, my senses were overwhelmed by the unforgettable stench of death. And that assault whenever I drove down Dekum Street did not dissipate over time.

There were gang shootings going on in that neighborhood, too. Granted, nobody ever shot at me, but you could hear the gunshots. There were nights I didn't want to stay in that house because of all the sirens and the shootings. I mean, I am over here! I live on the west side. Why would I go over there? Why would I go to Dekum Street?

I wrestled with that question, as did my wife and family. The answer, of which I was certainly aware, was one would have to be very deliberate to want to drive into inner Northeast Portland at night during that period of gang violence. And for a white man to create a relationship with a black man he didn't even know? That would take extreme intentionality. With purpose. And vulnerability. Or it would fail.

That concept of intentionality was a critical component to making those early racial reconciliation efforts work. Well, "work" is a debatable term. For weeks, and then months, and then years, me and a core group of black and white men made our way on Tuesday nights to the little yellow house where the elderly pastor and his wife lived. We met at seven p.m. and the conversation often went past nine, ten, or even eleven. It was terribly awkward at first.

Imagine a bunch of older white guys trying to "friend" a handful of younger black men. There were huge stereotypical walls to tear down. Trust was a big issue. Misunderstandings were prevalent. We had little in common, except for the fact most of us shared a faith in God. Spiritually, the black men and white men were aligned, but how that played out in our daily lives was very different. On Sundays—the most segregated day of the week—white families worshipped in their white churches in their respectable fashion, while black families in their black churches rollicked to gospel music amid loud exhortations. Different styles in honor of the same Savior. And, boy, did those differences carry over into the ways we communicated on Tuesday nights. The white guys were more reserved and usually played nice; the black guys often vented their anger and frustration. One group's language was refined, the other raw. Both reacted to hurt feelings—sometimes reservedly, sometimes loudly. Larry's best friend, Greg, a burly former college football player, told me he likens the Christian white man's admonishments to "Please, sir, will you refrain from that illicit activity? I am imploring you; please, stop." Or, he added, instead of using an offensive written word, whites would substitute with the phrase "expletive deleted."

But that's just not the way the black men communicated. Their style was raw, but not obscene. They called it "street talk." And for them it was normal everyday jargon; it was real. Those proclivities offended some of the white men who were turned off by the strong language. Sure, they might come once or twice, but the in-your-face confrontational approach that surfaced at times in the heat of the moment was not for everybody.

One of the guys who hung in there the longest—except for me and Larry—accused the black guys of being purposefully offensive, that by being so harsh and obtrusive they were testing whites, just to see if they would run. He developed what he called his "sacrifice of humility" to withstand what he considered their overbearing verbal assaults. Even though the guy's honesty was lauded in the group, his posturing could come across as pious to some.

Larry, who was still reeling from the rejections he had been experiencing in the name of religion, was more than annoyed. His frustration boiled over one night into a physical confrontation, known forevermore as the infamous "choke-hold ministry" incident. Larry doesn't deny he used a hands-on approach to make his point that evening; he just wanted to shut the guy up. "I'd been putting up with him and his insidiousness for a long time," Larry told us. "Because words didn't seem to mean anything to him, I thought it was time for him to experience a little sign language, with his feet off the ground." While we can laugh about that story today, I know Larry was not a happy camper at the time.

We were a couple years into this so-called reconciliation movement when I really began to question whether we were having any success. When my family and friends started pressing me about my ongoing participation, I didn't have a great answer, except to say I believed God didn't want me to quit. In fact, for more than a year I had been sparring with God over something I felt I was supposed to say to one specific person in that group. And maybe, just maybe, after delivering that message I might be set free.

CHAPTER FIFTEEN

Painful

I didn't think I would ever have to see those old white dudes again. Vic, maybe, but Wendell—no way. Victor was the opposite of what I thought about Wendell. He was this older guy with a very soothing voice; he obviously had a lot of compassion and he seemed sincere. He kinda reminded me of a father figure, and I listened to him. I couldn't have listened to Wendell. Wendell's words meant nothing to me. It was like somebody hitting me on the head with a rock. But Victor was very sweet, and he convinced me he believed what he was talking about. I thought he was a little misguided, but he was tolerable. If somebody had told me then Wendell and I would end up friends, I would have cussed them out and probably smacked them around some.

The thing is, Wendell and I both said reconciliation between us would never work. We didn't know it at the time, but we were just two idiot volunteers on a course that had been divinely orchestrated. And Waverly wouldn't drop the subject; he kept pushing for the conversation to continue. He was the one who was trying to carry the mantle of racial reconciliation in Portland at the time. He was the peacekeeper. Where there were gaps, he tried to build bridges. He even got a white man to join him on a weekly Christian radio talk show called "The Voice of Racial Reconciliation."

When Waverly finally talked me into starting a Tuesday night gathering of white men and black men to discuss how to improve race relations in Portland, I told him there was no way I was going to host it at my house. The first meeting there had been a disaster. And me and my friends aren't interested in going to a white location because that would mean the white guys would be in control of the meeting. Been there, done that. Black guys resent always having to be brought in to the white man's house because everything is scheduled at your time, at your convenience, with your friends. If we go to your house, you get the comfy chair and you always put us in the bad chair. Not gonna do that anymore.

We needed a neutral site where everyone would feel comfortable. A safe place where the memories of that first confrontation at my house would not be revisited. Fortunately, a local pastor and his wife offered to host. Pastor Ralph "Pop" Greenidge's house was centrally located—at least for me and my friends. We all grew up near there, went to school close by, played hoops, and caroused those streets. And I felt reasonably comfortable in that neighborhood because I patrolled those streets. Our so-called racial reconciliation movement kicked off at the Greenidge's home, which was located at the corner of Dekum and Twenty-Eighth, the innermost part of inner Northeast Portland—the heart of gang activity at the time.

But the "movement" didn't get off to a great start. I remember at one of those first Tuesday nights Vic asked one of the young black men if he believed the African-American community-at-large would be receptive to overtures from the white community. The guy shot down that notion with his answer: "With our people dodging bullets and not being able to pay rent, that wouldn't be high on our survival list, much less our priority list."

A second one tried to set Victor straight by pointing out another major problem—actually two: "Vic, you need to understand two things about black males—two problems most blacks in Portland face every day. The first problem is anger. And the second problem is white males."

Man, those early interactions with the white guys were painful. I mean PAINFUL! Ralph was a really nice guy, and his wife put up with a lot, but it was excruciating at times. Here were these white heads with all their religious talk, blabbing on and on about stuff I don't give a crap about: "Oh, we should be friends." "We should go on retreats." And then I got my black guys who won't say what they really feel to these white guys. That's what we do, we hide ourselves from white guys. So we're all sitting around doing these little platitudes. And after a while I'm just boiling.

At that time in my life I was pretty much mad at everything and everybody. I was angry because I couldn't protect the kids in my neighborhood from gang violence. I was upset with the black church leadership because they had abdicated their role as caretakers of their community. I felt ostracized from my fellow police officers. And white people? They just didn't give a rip about young black boys dying.

I hadn't given up on God...yet, but I found myself challenging the man upstairs to start showing up. Or else. I was dealing with craziness every day, and I was thinking, "God, if you don't save me, then there ain't no God and nobody is going to be saved, so maybe I should just go out and kill as many people as I can because I got to bring attention to this; I got to stop this."

I knew something had to change, or I was going to be dead. I was either going to die or be killed, or I was going to kill somebody. I knew I wouldn't kill myself, but the reckless attitude I adopted led to borderline suicidal behavior. I would barge into known gang houses by myself. I would challenge gang-bangers to fights. I would insert myself into extremely volatile situations—without any backup. But amazingly in my career as a cop I never fired my weapon in the line of duty.

This potentially self-destructive conduct came at a critical time in my life, a phase where everything I thought I knew about life and humanity had been turned upside down. I was supposed to be one of the good guys, a cop whose job was to protect people and save lives. But kids were dying left and right. The church, the community? They were supposed to come alongside as a solution, not become more of the problem. I couldn't even prevent my partner's son from getting killed in a gang shooting.

Later, I would learn my anger at that time was a secondary response to my fear of abandonment. The life I had chosen was designed to protect kids and save lives, but that dream had been shattered. I felt exposed, vulnerable. Doubts and fears flooded my psyche. From that the anger flowed.

Fortunately for the rest of the world, I spent a lot of time by myself in my police car. That's where I started to have these "heart-to-hearts" with the Lord. Sometimes they were quiet prayerful conversations. Other times I would vent my frustrations aloud. I had a lot of questions. About life. And my purpose for that life.

I questioned my role as a so-called leader of African-American men who had been meeting with white guys to hash out our racial differences. It seemed like a colossal waste of time! These dudes were so full of apathy. They lived in this dream world unaware of black kids dying in my neighborhood. After a while I couldn't see them, I couldn't hear them.

That was my state of mind on a particular Tuesday when I had to respond to yet another gang shooting—this one at Thirtieth and Sumner in Northeast Portland. It was just a few blocks from Pop Greenidge's house where a bunch of white guys and some of my black friends were headed later that night.

When I arrived at the crime scene, a sixteen-year-old African-American boy lay dead in the street. Gunned down by a rival gang member in the middle of the day. It was an all-too-common incident, not unlike the dozens of shootings and teen killings I had been assigned to investigate over the past several months.

But this one was different. I wasn't just going through the motions anymore, emotionally detached like I had taught myself to be for so long. No, I had changed. Ever since my partner's son's death in a drive-by shooting, I took every young kid's murder on my watch personally. It hurt deep down. And I wanted answers.

After they took the bloodied body away, I stood over the chalk outline for a long while. Alone now with my thoughts, I remember asking God a simple question: "Why?" I wasn't surprised there was no answer. At that moment I wasn't even sure God existed. It wasn't that I didn't believe in God, I just didn't believe he would do anything about what was happening to us because we had disqualified ourselves. We lived like he didn't exist; so why should God do anything for us?

I was already an hour late when I drove the couple of blocks over to Greenidge's house. I parked my patrol car out front, but I didn't get out. I would have usually driven back to the precinct to clean up and change clothes before the meeting. But here I was—with blood on my uniform, sweaty from being outside all afternoon, emotionally charged, but physically and spiritually drained.

I was sitting out in the car trying to convince myself not to go in there. I was so bent out of shape because those white guys didn't give a crap about us. Did they even care another young black kid just got killed down the street? Is there anything white people are going to tell me that is going to solve my problem? No, there's nothing they could do or say that was going to change the situation. And that made me even angrier. So I screamed. At God. Again.

"God, what am I supposed to do?! Who am I supposed to be? Cuz this crap is crazy, and I can't take any more of this. What do you want me to do?"

There was only silence. I waited a few more minutes, but nothing. I was so worked up I didn't feel like going home. So I got out of the car and strode into Pop Greenidge's house—an hour-and-a-half late. Most of the guys had already left, but Wendell had stuck around. Maybe for no other reason than to nag me about my tardiness. As soon as I walked through that door, Wendell started in: "Why can't you black guys ever be on time?" he whined.

CHAPTER SIXTEEN

Love That Man

As different as Larry and I were, we both shared a passion for the law. I was at the height of my career during the time we were meeting at Greenidge's, managing eight to ten major criminal defense cases at the same time. And while I never represented any of the people Larry arrested on murder charges, he was a very gang-savvy cop who kept a lot of criminal defense attorneys busy. Portland during the early nineties was just an extremely active time for law enforcement and law firms. A lot of tension. A lot of stress.

That all boiled over one Tuesday evening at Pop's house. On my drive down Dekum I remember seeing a lot of cop cars in the middle of the street a couple blocks from where we met. Probably another gang shooting, I surmised. And I figured Anderson had to be involved somehow. I got there about ten to seven like I usually did—I have this thing about not being late. In addition to Larry's friends, Greg and Leonard, I think there were two or three white guys there as well. We all kind of assumed Larry wouldn't be joining us because it was after eight-thirty and the group was starting to break up.

I was kind of surprised and put out when Larry walked in about eight-forty-five. I think I made some sarcastic comment about his chronic tardiness—and then immediately regretted the poke. Because here was this six-foot-six-inch, 280-pound man marching toward me. I was very aware now that the stern-looking officer was still in uniform, was soaked with sweat, and had dried blood on his sleeves. But it was the wild look in his eyes that scared me most.

He immediately laid into me, demanding to know what I was going to do about another young black kid dead on the street. Did I even care about gangs and all the killings in his neighborhood? He cursed at me and ranted about racism in America and how I was part of the problem. By this time, the furious cop was standing over me as I sank lower into the couch, his finger in my face, commanding me to respond to some pretty open-ended questions. First of all, I remember thinking, if Larry Anderson was going to be a part of this, it can't work. Because I was afraid of him, and it seemed he was making me afraid on purpose. And as far as coming up with the right answer—whatever that might be in the angry man's mind—well, I had nothing. So, when Larry prodded me again, I gave an honest answer: "Nothing! I'm not going to do anything about black kids dying. And I'm not going to do anything about racism."

With his face about twelve inches from mine, I could easily see the pathetic smirk. "I knew it, I knew it!" he exulted as he spun around in front of me in some weird dance of satisfaction, adding, "That's exactly what I thought! You ain't goin' to do nothin'."

But when he turned around and was in my face again, I made another confession, this one barely audible: "No, I can't do anything about that; I can only do what God told me to do."

That declaration lit a fire under the feet of the already amped-up cop. As he strutted around the room in front of the few shocked faces that hadn't yet exited the back door, he started mocking me, accusing

me of being this righteous white man who undoul
tentious religious bullshit-of-a-revelation to annou

He taunted me over my claim I had received
Almighty. I could tell he was ready to pounce i
satisfy his urge to heap further condemnation on my head. So he basically ordered me to relay the message—adding I was to share with the
assembled "*exactly* what God told you to do, Wendell."

He didn't have to add "or else" to the directive; I knew I was facing
dire consequences if he wasn't satisfied. So I slowly stood up, gathered
myself, and in my strongest voice said, "He told me...to love you."

CHAPTER SEVENTEEN

Murder on My Mind

Whooooosh! It felt like all the air just rushed out of Pop Greenidge's front room. Wendell's totally unexpected retort completely deflated my tirade.

Telling me he loved me hit me like a sack of bricks. Like somebody threw cold water on my hot temperament. Here I was going off on him, ready to prove my points—point one, point two—and then he says something like that. First of all, I wasn't ready for it, so it kinda took me back a little bit. I'd never heard a man say it to another man; never knew of any white guy to say it to a black guy.

Just minutes earlier I had been outside on the porch, my temperament peaking at "DEFCON-One-More-Thing." And when Wendell needled me about my late arrival—after I'd been out all afternoon on yet another gang killing—I definitely had murder on my mind. If he hadn't come up with the right answer at the right moment in that front room, Wendell might have been one dead attorney.

Looking back, I realize what an unstable, scary dude I had become. But I was totally unaware of it at the time. In that heated moment I wasn't in my right mind. And I wasn't exactly sure what I was capable of doing if one more hot button got pushed. And then Wendell and his holier-than-thou attitude pushed me over the edge.

He was more worried about the clock on the wall than another kid getting shot and killed. He didn't even know where the black kids were. He didn't care they were dying all around me. To me in my fury he represented every brick wall I had been running into. And I was itching to knock down that wall. I demanded to know what Wendell was going to do about the killings. What was he going to do about racism? And I swore to him if he didn't say the right answer, then that's the wrong answer, and there was going to be a problem.

And then he came up with the only answer I could have heard. If anybody else would have said that, I wouldn't have believed it. But how could this man—who I know was scared to death of me, who didn't know how this was going to work out, who was not in control—say "I love you" to me at that moment when everybody else had run off? All I know is I heard God speak through Wendell; that was God speaking to me.

Wendell was the vessel God used to reach deep down inside me. Here I was on the brink of hopelessness, but in that moment of spiritual intervention God showed me I had not been abandoned. I had not been forgotten. I was loved.

That night I had been acting like a mad man, and none of the other guys tried to interrupt my outburst. In fact, when I composed myself and looked around, they were all gone. I tried to regain some of my swagger by letting Wendell know the burden of proof of what had happened that night was on the white guy:

"That's another promise from you and everybody else who, when it gets hot, you ain't never going to be around. Hell, I bet you ain't going to be around the rest of the day. We'll see, Wendell, we'll see."

God must have had a grand sense of humor to pair opposites like me and Wendell Birkland. I would have never picked Wendell because he represented everything I hated about white people—he was arrogant, aloof, indignant. But that's how the two of us knew God was in charge. Neither would have chosen the other. God selected us; we didn't get to pick each other.

In the weeks and months following that life-changing encounter, I felt encouraged about a closer relationship with my Heavenly Father. And I believed through Wendell God had answered my prayer. It was like God said, "Finally! Are you ready to do what I told you to do a long time ago? You cannot do it by yourself. Are you ready now?" I had nothing to say at that moment, but I also knew I had nothing to offer. I was essentially telling God I didn't have anything else in me if he didn't keep showing up. I didn't have a Plan B.

Me and Wendell stayed committed to building a relationship across racial lines, but everyone else in that group eventually moved on. And then I got approached by the Boy Scouts to see if I could fill in for one of their leaders who had dropped out. The troop met on Tuesday nights, so I told Pop, Wendell, and the others that our dwindling racial reconciliation movement was done. I was moving on.

PART THREE

UNITED

CHAPTER EIGHTEEN

Bad Boy Scouts

When Larry declared an end to the racial reconciliation meetings, I thought I might be off the hook. This could be my opportunity to reclaim Tuesday nights, maybe find some new friends. But after a couple days thinking about my commitment to the man, I called Larry. I let him know I was going to be his assistant Scout leader.

For more than a year prior, I had resisted God's nudging me to tell Larry he was loved. I don't know why I fought so hard to just be obedient and share God's love with him; maybe it had something to do with my prayerful rebuttal that got in the way: "Lord, why couldn't you give me a black friend like Leonard Lamberth or Greg Taylor instead of an angry black dude with a gun?"

Turns out the man with little hope needed to hear those words. But just because a white guy told a black guy "I love you" didn't mean everything would be rosy. In fact, things got worse. I don't know if Larry was trying to test me or what, but I was clearly on the receiving end of a whole lot of "I'm-going-to-beat-the-crap-out-of-you-and-we'll-see-if-you-really-love-me stuff." Larry wanted to know if I would stand by him. I wasn't going to change the world. I wasn't going to tear down the gate and move. I was going to love him, but I really didn't know what that looked like working. All I knew was Larry was making my revelation extremely difficult to sustain. Actually, I was more afraid of what that might mean going forward. I knew it wasn't going to be easy.

Larry was being very hostile at that time. He acted like a warrior in the midst of the battle. And, frankly, I didn't want to share any part of my life with him. I didn't hate him; hating would be wrong. I just didn't want to be with him.

But that obedience thing caused me to think twice—and pray more—when given the opportunity to end my relationship with Larry. By volunteering to be his assistant Boy Scout leader, I believed I was being faithful to God's leading. But that didn't mean I had figured out what God meant when he impressed upon me to "Love that man." For the longest time, I had tried on my own strength to treat Larry like a pal, a buddy in the legal system I could joke around with, a cop with whom I could share some friendly banter. But with that approach there was no reciprocity. The guy was just a huge nut to crack.

Larry had this big shell around him, which prevented anyone from penetrating and hurting him. Man, he could keep you away, too. And it wasn't like I warmed up to him either because he never showed a chink in the armor, no hint of compassion or weakness.

But the one thing I couldn't escape was the truth from the Scriptures, the part where Jesus says the greatest commandment is to "Love the Lord your God with all your heart and with all your soul and with all your mind." And the second is like it: "Love your neighbor as yourself." Of course, the lawyer in me wanted to debate who my neighbor was. But I knew that meant my fellow man; that meant African Americans and others whose skin color was different than mine. I also knew Larry had a heart after God, and since the Scriptures say, "Whoever does God's will is my brother..." Larry was, according to the Bible, my brother. But warm up to somebody like Larry Anderson? That didn't seem possible. So for me it all boiled down to being obedient...or not. I believed Larry was my neighbor, my brother. And I believed—but didn't totally understand why—God wanted me to love that man. It was up to me to do my faithful best and figure it out from there.

With a man like Larry, love isn't gushy, it's not emotional. Love is consistency. I really thought the best way for me to love him was to be his friend, to be with him, to really get to know him enough that I could grow in respect for him.

So I bought the Boy Scout Handbook—but not the khaki shorts—and with Larry attempted a crash course on skills we didn't possess. We were terrible at tying knots, awful at leather and bead work, and didn't know the first thing about Pinewood Derbies or merit badges. We were two inept Scout leaders. I mean, there were some real deficiencies in our abilities.

We were so bad at it the troop nearly disintegrated. When I brought my son, Ryan, to bolster attendance at one of the meetings, only one other kid showed up. Ryan called me out and jabbed me with, "Maybe you should change the name from Boy Scouts to Boy Scout."

As disastrous as it was, Larry and I persevered for a couple of years. And along the way something amazing happened. Previously, we had barely tolerated each other, but as we devoted more time to playing Boy Scout leaders we discovered we actually liked hanging out together. Like the entire day we spent on a field trip building snow caves on Mt. Hood. Turns out we were building unity, too.

Larry and I were becoming friends, but we weren't the only two men in Oregon who were trying to bridge the gap between whites and blacks. Sure, we had terminated our feisty version of "racial reconciliation" for a term as Boy Scout leaders, but there were other attempts—more peaceful ones—initiated in Portland to foster friendly relations between white men and others of different skin color. That was clearly evident following the big Promise Keepers rally in Boulder, Colorado. A parade of white guys from Portland—many stuffed into stinky RVs—came home exhausted but spiritually on fire to live up to the Seven Promises speakers like James Dobson, E.V. Hill, and Jack Hayford emphasized. One of the promises Coach Bill McCartney—the leader of the national men's movement—exhorted the 50,000 cheering attendees to uphold was, "A Promise Keeper is committed to reaching beyond any racial and denominational barriers to demonstrate the power of biblical unity."

Inspired by the Coach's message and challenged by the lack of outreach to minorities during the inaugural Oregon Vision, a group of white guys started walking the talk. They bought a slew of tickets to the annual Civil War football game between the University of Oregon Ducks and the Oregon State Beavers and shared half of them with some African-American men they wanted to hang out with. They supported an outreach in the black community called Jesus Against Drugs and Alcohol. They prayed over black leaders and pastors at an all-night campout in an African-American church in North Portland. They hosted retreats at a cabin on Mt. Hood, made memorable by a white businessman who ceremoniously washed the feet of the black men in an act of contrition and submission. They invited speakers to share their views on racial reconciliation and opened the presentations to the Northeast Portland community. The speakers included Lee Mun Wah who produced the documentary *The Color of Fear* about the state of race relations in America; and Joel Freeman, Chaplain for the Washington Wizards, who wrote *Return to Glory*, a history of the black race.

The African-American contingent being courted by the white guys included a businessman, some city employees, a community activist, and some pastors, but their numbers dwindled as the strain of organizing events by white people for black people became palpable. Contrived? Probably. But the white lawyers, accountants, and business owners who were trying to be good promise keepers were doing their best based on what they knew. No minorities part of Oregon Vision? No problem, the next event we host they'll get an invitation. Separated by racial barriers? Let's go to a football game and sit on the same side. Don't understand our differences? Easy, we'll bring in another speaker. The white guys really stretched when they identified an opportunity for a Caucasian to go into business with an African American, with financial backing from a team of white investors. Unfortunately, the venture failed miserably and left a trail of bad feelings.

It was this type of rancor that spun me and Larry back into the orbit of race relations. It had been three years since Larry had given up on the white dudes who had tried to shove their brand of racial reconciliation down his throat. But now, a few of those men who had stepped in and out of Tuesday nights at the Greenidge's were regrouping in the small office of an African-American businessman...and Larry and I felt compelled to participate.

Initially, the new group of six—three blacks and three whites—formed to pray for the development of a Portland Business Luncheon in the city's close-in Northeast area, one designed to be more culturally diverse than the other monthly gatherings on the west side, which were attended mainly by whites. But before me and Larry jumped in too deep, we offered up some ground rules. The guidelines were based on lessons we had learned the hard way in the first go-round: Past failures had to be recognized and reconciled before any real progress could be made. And reconciliation would not be possible unless it was founded on personal relationships.

Larry and I didn't need another project to work on or another meeting to attend—although we eventually abandoned our Bad Boy

Scout leader gigs—and we certainly weren't interested in going down a similar dead-end path that had led to those weekly volatile encounters at the Greenidge's home. No, if this core group of three black men and three white men was going to survive, there were some past failures that needed to be faced. And who better than Mr. Anderson to shine his big ol' policeman's flashlight on some ugly dark stuff no one wanted to look at?

CHAPTER NINETEEN

No Plan B

The "racial reconciliation" fiasco at Pop's had fizzled out and I had happily moved on to the Boy Scouts. But I was still smarting from the years-long excruciating experience and the unresolved effort. I had hated seeing whitey after whitey march into the Greenidge residence with their religious spirits and ministry mentality, trying to fix whatever they felt was wrong with us black guys. It was agonizing just being in each other's presence! We couldn't get past ourselves, our personalities, playing our roles—those were all barriers God needed to break down. And the demolition process took years.

God said, "All you guys coming in here with your walls built up and your big ol' housing structures under construction, it's time for a tearing down. Everybody bring your sledgehammer and just bash each other's stuff down."

It was a period of time I look back on as The Wrecking Crew Assembly. And, of course, I had the biggest hammer, so I was the focal point for all that devastation and destruction. And I was good at it. Religiosity was bashed. Personal agendas were obliterated. Superiority, prejudice, false humility, pride, privilege—stripped down to the studs. When the dust had cleared after the collective tearing down and dismantling of pretenses, the foundation of our "racial reconciliation" effort was barely intact. Only me and Wendell were left to pick up the pieces.

And I have to admit I was kind of surprised Wendell stuck around and followed me over to the Boy Scouts. It had been a rocky start for us, considering the blowup over the Cliff Robinson incident nearly a decade earlier and the escalating encounters between the two of us at the stalled "racial reconciliation" debacle. But the time we shared doing the Boy Scout thing gave me and Wendell a chance to get to know one another a little better. We actually heard each other for the first time. We started listening to each other's opinions. And, as time went by, we developed more of a personal relationship. We actually started becoming friends.

We got to know each other's families. We shared meals together. We intentionally sought out each other's company at community events and gatherings. And we had fun together! But sometimes I tell Wendell I don't even know why I like him. The guy can't hoop, he's old, he's got these crazy old ideas, and he lives in a gated community. We laugh about it; it's funny now. But it wasn't funny then. It was tragic.

But if Wendell hadn't been in my life, how would God have saved me with a lifeline? After that supernatural experience, it was as if the scales had fallen from my eyes and I began to see people as they were—broken and in need of Jesus. Not as I had perceived them to be in church leadership, not as I had stereotyped them to be on the police force, not as I wanted them to be—immune from the violence in the community where I grew up. That change of heart first manifested itself at my work where, as God began to piece my life back together, I became aware of the fallenness of those I encountered. That period in my career also coincided with a major change in duties.

I had technically been on leave from the Portland Police Bureau while I served as the G.R.E.A.T. coordinator, a position that required extensive travel, training, and education. And I was at the top of my game: I drove a Corvette emblazoned with G.R.E.A.T. on it; the program I ran was the most

successful of all run by the ATF; and I was respected by my peers. Plus, I had
been invited to make more than 100 presentations over the years detailing
my approach to gang prevention methods. In my mind I was famous for my
achievements. But all the so-called fame came at a cost. There was the busy
schedule that kept me on the road, sometimes up to three weeks out of
the month—and this at a time when Renee and I had adopted a son, Kaleb.
And even though there was a lot of ground-breaking gang prevention work
being done, I just wasn't feeling the impact on the streets of Portland.

Alone one day at a conference in Las Vegas, I wrestled with my disillu-
sionment, and as I reflected on where I was personally, professionally, and
spiritually at that moment in my life, I felt God's urging for me to quit. It
wasn't a sense I should quit working, but that I needed to stop pumping
myself up, quit relying on my own good works, and turn back to total reli-
ance on my Heavenly Father.

Sitting there in that suite in the Rio, I was thinking I was at the pinnacle
of my career, the posterchild for the ATF, but I told God all I wanted was more
of him and less of me. I felt him saying, "Trust me," so when I got back home
I resigned my position.

That didn't go over well with my superiors. ATF sent some feds out to
try to talk me into staying, but to no avail. And the Portland Police Bureau
administration considered my resignation a slap in the face because of the
unrealized potential benefit from the work I had been doing—like the negotiations I had been involved with to build a G.R.E.A.T. training center in Oregon,
a win that would have generated millions of dollars and positive press. But
after I quit that project went nowhere. Now there was only embarrassment.

I went back to being a cop in uniform, and a lonely one at that. My fellow
officers ostracized me and criticized me for being a quitter, taunting me with
accusations I must have done something terribly wrong, that I was never
qualified in the first place, that they had known from the beginning there
was something wrong with me. They avoided me like the plague, like I had

leprosy. The image of myself associated with G.R.E.A.T. was removed from all marketing materials, billboards, and bus ads. They even took my name off an annual award that had been created in my honor. It was humiliating. No one, including my commanders, wanted to acknowledge Officer Larry Anderson even existed. It felt awful showing up in that work environment. I hated every day of it. But I refused to defend my decision. It was something I had worked out with God, and I was going to trust the experience would prepare me for something even greater.

I didn't try to explain myself or justify my decision because it was a test. I believed God didn't want me to claim my success with G.R.E.A.T. had anything to do with my own abilities. And I would have failed that test if my will and pride had persisted because I would have disqualified myself from being trusted in the future to do God's will and give him the glory.

That trying time was a humbling experience, one of the most difficult but important episodes of my life. For the first time I could remember, I became insignificant. For years my identity had been tied to law enforcement's efforts to combat Portland's gang problem. But now I was no longer a member of the Gang Enforcement Team; my term as Gang Intelligence Officer over.

I used to be "the man," but as a regular patrol officer I felt like this forgotten guy nobody wanted to see or be seen with. I was kind of in this lull, where all I did for years was go to work, come home, work, and come home. But there was a certain element of the population that hadn't forgotten about me.

Even though I was technically out of the gang business, my reputation as a tough-on-crime gang fighter had not diminished. To the Bloods and Crips, the only change they recognized was I no longer wore jeans and a shirt—the way I had dressed on the gang unit. Now I was awfully conspicuous in my blue uniform with the shiny badge on it as I patrolled the streets of North/Northeast Portland by myself. It was common knowledge I had made several enemies along the way with my brash style and combative approach. And the word on the street was there were some scores to settle.

I knew of at least two people who had publicly promised they were going to kill me—one was a violent, mentally unstable man named Sam who disappeared; the other, Michael Fesser, was a shot-caller for the Woodlawn Bloods. After jacking up one of his Blood associates at a car wash one afternoon, I encountered Michael on the street and he professed his hatred toward me. While no guns were pulled, threats were made. And when we agreed to part with "I'll see you later," both of us knew from then on it was all about time, place, and opportunity. We each understood the next confrontation would end in gunfire.

But, probably fortunately for both of us, Michael got yanked off the streets because of a busted drug deal and spent two years in prison. When he got out, he apparently had had a change of heart and disavowed his gang affiliation. I knew nothing about Michael's transformation, so when I ran into him at a Chipotle restaurant one day, I carefully pulled my gun out of its holster and put it in my right-hand pants pocket, thinking the "I'll-see-you-later" time had arrived. I was on full alert as Michael walked up to me and said, "Hey, man, why you looking at me like that? Did I do something to upset you?"

I kept my hand on my gun and didn't relax because, even though it had been more than two years, I didn't believe Michael had forgotten about our previous run-in. I dropped my guard a bit after Michael apologized for his past discretions and invited me to church.

I dropped one of my skeptical "We'll see" comments, but weeks later I did seek Michael out at his church. After the service I walked over to him and he seemed kind of nervous. I told him he was the reason I was there and he had nothing to worry about anymore. As I turned to go, I noticed a tear fall down his cheek. Years later Michael started a prison ministry. I'm proud to say I support his ministry with my time and resources.

Mentoring young African-American men—whether Knuckleheads, Boy Scouts, summer basketball players involved with the Police Activities League, or former gang members trying to reclaim their lives—had always been on

157

my heart. And because I was feeling excommunicated by my fellow police officers at the time, I seriously considered resigning and going into some kind of mentoring or ministry work. I was all set to cash in on my nearly twenty years on the force when I unexpectedly got offered a job in Personnel. We had a new African-American police chief who wanted my help recruiting and hiring more minorities. I thought maybe the Personnel desk would be a good place to finish off my career. I told my wife I would give it a year.

As I contemplated my future beyond police work, my prayer was that God would reveal ministry opportunities with young, at-risk men in my African-American community. Boy, was I surprised when I felt led to minister to the men and women of the Portland Police Bureau.

I believe God was showing me there's hurting people all around. I saw them in the locker room where I could count three lockers belonging to officers who had killed themselves with their own guns. Police have high suicide rates, high divorce rates, high alcoholism rates. God impressed upon me that I didn't have to go "out" and minister; I just had to reach over to the person next to me.

So, anyone who came to my office would receive an encouraging word—nothing religious—just something like, "You can make it"; "Just hang in there one more day"; "Don't worry about it, things will get better." I even earned a new reputation—I became known as "that crazy police minister." Of course, it got me into trouble with my administration, but I was beyond caring about getting promoted—or even fired, for that matter. I was in Personnel, after all, so I felt offering a kind word to my peers or even offering to pray for them was the right thing to do. I only balked when I started doubting my qualifications to "go minister to those white dudes," as I firmly believed God was directing me to do. I hadn't gone to seminary, wasn't a theologian, and had no church sanctions. But I did study the Scriptures and tried my best to listen to God's promptings. What I felt led to do at the time was to make the Portland Police Bureau my ministerial training ground.

Of course, I realized I had crossed a threshold when I committed to following God's plan by becoming a "pseudo minister" within the department. There would be no turning back. No Plan B. And I was actually fine with that. Ever since I had heard through Wendell that God was mindful of me, my faith had increased season over season.

I don't want to have a Plan B, because when you got options you really don't give your all to Plan A. I have willfully given up the prospect I have a choice when it comes to doing God's will. Some might feel restricted to live without a Plan B, C, D, E, or F, but I felt free. And God rewarded my faithfulness several months into my new role when he nudged me to check how many gang-related homicides had occurred since I had stopped patrolling the streets. There had been one.

I remember thinking that couldn't be possible. But after I looked back at everything God had been doing, I realized he's the one who saves communities—not men, not me. When you do what you're supposed to do, then God does what he wants to do. And he rescues and saves your people.

I was a pseudo minister without a Plan B. And God had me exactly where he wanted me. It was a training ground that would prepare me for my most demanding assignment yet: to lead a cross-cultural relationship-building movement that would take me to Washington, DC; Africa; and back home to Portland, Oregon, where God wanted me to confront racism and religiosity in the whitest, most unchurched state in America.

CHAPTER TWENTY

Ambassadors of Reconciliation

The unlikely friendship between me—an older white criminal defense attorney—and a younger African-American police officer became a topic of conversation in certain circles around Portland as we "went public" with our relationship. We didn't chase publicity, but the media paid attention whenever we made presentations at area churches or spoke at public venues. One reporter, who was covering one of our talks at a Martin Luther King Day event, wrote, "In spite of their rocky start, the two are as close as friends can be, lending one another support and respect, spending time together, and sharing their message of friendship."

And then there was one Christmas when I gave my testimony before a crowd of more than five hundred at a businessmen's luncheon in downtown Portland. I had asked Larry to introduce me, and I'll never forget what he said. He described me as a guy like the Tin Man in *The Wizard of Oz*—someone who already had the most love of all but wished he could care more and do more for his friends. And then he turned to me and said, "Wendell, it's because of you, who has demonstrated to me what love is all about, that I am a changed man. You're the Tin Man—you had the heart the whole time, dude."

We almost didn't make it to one of our scheduled speeches at a Baptist church one April Sunday because my dad was on his death bed in a Portland hospital. When I told Larry Dad was dying and I needed to cancel, he demurred. He said we would both go, or neither would go. And he reminded me of a specific Scripture that states, "Anyone who loves their father or mother more than me is not worthy of me; anyone who loves their son or daughter more than me is not worthy of me." I thought Larry was being harsh and insensitive, but after a quick run to the hospital my mom convinced me to go because she felt there was nothing anyone could do for Dad. So we made our presentation on reconciliation. And my father passed away five days later.

Larry's position was God knew Dad was sick, and he knew the day he would pass—nothing any of us could do about it. And God worked out the details. We kept our promise and made the presentation, and Dad died the next Friday with all of us there.

But our unique bond took a dramatic turn when I invited Larry to join me in representing the state of Oregon at a National Prayer Breakfast in Washington, DC. I had been to several of them before and—just like my Oregon Vision experience years before—I noticed a pattern of whiteness there. I didn't expect to have a forum to speak out about the lack of diversity, but when I was asked last minute to fill in for a moderator at one of the breakout sessions, I went "off script" and challenged the room full of some 250 white people:

"One thing I would like to bring up with you folks is you have all been invited to this prayer breakfast by somebody, probably the person sitting next to you," my spur-of-the-moment sermon began in the bowels of the Washington Hilton. "And that's what we encourage, you know, to invite people here out of relationship. Well, if you notice, this room is all white. There is only one black man in the room."

As all heads craned to see who I was pointing out in the back of the room, I continued: "That's my friend, Larry Anderson, standing back there. Larry has come because I invited him. I wanted him to be here. I believe this place should be different. If you folks would go back home and invite others, it would be different. This place would be different. Your lives would be different. I think God wants that."

The room went silent as I stepped away from my temporary pulpit, a response assuring me I would never again be given a microphone at a presidential prayer gathering made up of all white people. As I made my way to the back of the room, the awkward moment was strained even further by the angry stare on Larry's face. Later, after I reminded him it was he who had said real friends can embarrass each other in public, Larry softened. Now that we had cemented our relationship as "real friends," we could both expect there would be a whole lot of embarrassing each other in public from then on. Because, unspoken or not, we believed our bond had been sealed in heaven. We were convinced we would be around "until...," which was Larry's favorite way of indicating our demise or the arrival of Kingdom Come.

I thought I might have alienated myself from the good folks at the National Prayer Breakfast with my impromptu lecture about race relations, but through personal connections my wife and I made there we established friendships around the world. Of course, we knew Doug Coe from the Oregon Vision experience, and he loved nothing more than putting people from diverse backgrounds together.

Our world got rocked when Kristi and I were asked if we would host Benazir Bhutto, a Muslim who was then Prime Minister of Pakistan. When Doug called, it wasn't like, "Well, this guy's a Catholic, this one's a Muslim, she's a Protestant; what do you think?" He didn't care what church you went to. He was all about pushing everyone to have relationships with people all over the world. I mean, here's Benazir, a Muslim woman, and she stayed with us; we became friends.

There were others who stayed with us, including a Buddhist monk from Mongolia who sought to acclimatize to American customs with two very unusual requests. The monk—in full red-robe regalia—asked my wife to take him shopping so he could buy an outfit for his wife (yes, Kristi learned, some Buddhist monks can marry). She drove him to the local mall and helped him pick out a Pendleton blazer with "Made in Oregon" on it. Later I took the monk out for lunch and asked if there was anything else he needed. He thanked me and said there was something: the monk wanted to know where he could buy some pornography. I delicately declined to facilitate that request; it wasn't a custom I was interested in perpetuating.

Another time, when Coe's longtime friend, Pierre Buyoya—the president of Burundi—wanted to start a prayer breakfast in his East African country, a call went out for volunteers from our National Prayer Breakfast to attend. My wife and I were acquainted with the new U.S. Ambassador to the Republic of Burundi, so we went with them. It definitely wasn't a vacation given there was a civil war going on, but we felt somewhat safe because we got to stay at the Ambassador's house.

When pressed to explain the purpose of that first Burundi National Prayer Breakfast, I told the Ambassador it was all about reconciliation. President Buyoya's hope was, through prayer, relations between the warring Hutus and Tutsis could be restored. I told the Ambassador a number of politicians—including representatives of both enemy factions—would be attending the prayer breakfast. The Ambassador asked for, and received, an invitation. In fact, she was asked to speak to the assembly at the dinner following the breakfast. Because the entire prayer breakfast thing was new to her, she asked me if I could suggest some good words. I directed her to the story in the Scriptures about the wise man who built his house on the rock. She used those Bible verses in her talk on peace and reconciliation at the nation's first national prayer gathering.

When we were invited back the next year, many—including the Ambassador—advised we not go. Rebels had attacked the capital, we were told, and it was too dangerous. But President Buyoya was persistent. He so wanted the American reconcilers to come to his country's second prayer breakfast he put us up in a safe hotel and paid the bill. I was even asked to speak to the assembled Hutus and Tutsis.

It was one of the most difficult things I've ever had to do. These guys had been killing each other for years—ethnic fighting between the Hutus and Tutsis had killed more than 150,000—and there were generations of hatred between them. What could I say or do to promote reconciliation? I decided to go with the parable of the Good Samaritan, in which an expert in the law asked Jesus how he could inherit eternal life. Jesus told him to love God and love his neighbor, but the man questioned who his neighbor was. I took some liberties with the players in the story, but they got the point:

> Jesus replied that a Tutsi man was going down from Jerusalem to Jericho. He fell upon robbers. They stripped him and beat him, went off leaving him half dead. By chance, a Catholic priest was going down that road. When he saw the Tutsi on the ground, he passed by on the other side. Then a Mormon came to the same place, and he passed by on the other side. But a Hutu who was on the journey, saw him, felt compassion, and bandaged him up.

After a pause I asked the Hutus and Tutsis who they thought was a neighbor to the Tutsi man who had fallen into the hand of robbers.

"The Hutu, the one who had mercy on him," they all agreed.

"Yes," I replied. "And you know what Jesus said at the end of the parable? 'Go and do likewise.'"

I haven't been back to Burundi since that second prayer breakfast—the place is just too dangerous. But I haven't forgotten the challenge I left with the Hutus and Tutsis: "Love God and love your neighbor as yourself." That's because I've had my own struggles with trying to answer the question, "Who is my neighbor?"

To me, the question is more like, "Who do I *have* to love? Who do I really have to love?" If I'm a Tutsi, do I have to love this Hutu that for generations has destroyed my family? If a Hutu, do I have to love this Tutsi that killed my son, killed my daughter?

The concept is simple: love God, love others. Simple. Simple, but hard. If you are Hutu and you are Tutsi, simple, but it's hard. If you are a politician, love God, love your neighbor, but what if he's on the other side of the aisle? As a white guy, do I have to love this black jerk who's being mean to me? Simple, but hard.

Larry and I had bashed each other's heads in for years, trying in our own power to figure each other out and overcome our differences. It wasn't until I finally surrendered my will and submitted to God's leading that the two of us merged onto the road of reconciliation. I was well aware of the cost of such an endeavor. It was an expensive courting process, one that took tons of time and a supreme commitment to keep showing up, even when we didn't want to, even when nobody else did.

Commitment is one of the first things that impressed me about Larry. Especially with his friends—total commitment. For me, my tendency was to be your friend for a period of time, but if it becomes too difficult or costly, I move on. But I didn't move on from my expensive relationship with Larry, not because of the cost—I stayed because of its value. We persevered because we both believed God had ordained it, making that bond way too valuable to break.

CHAPTER TWENTY-ONE

Back Together Again

I'm an all-or-nothing guy, so when it came time to dive back into the world of so-called racial reconciliation I wanted to go deep—or nowhere at all. I wasn't interested in dealing again with a bunch of white guys who were oblivious to the past. We needed to collectively face up to the fact this country was founded on the subjugation of one group for the benefit of the other. So there's never been a point in our history where black and white men were ever on the same equal playing field. Now, there was a time prior to the slave trade when blacks were in this country as free men alongside whites, but there was never "conciliation" between them—only business relationships. Without conciliation between whites and blacks, there can be no such thing as racial "reconciliation."

And when we go back to the beginning, we learn the identity of race is fraud—it has no foundation. God doesn't address white/black. There's no distinction between white and black apart from what our cultural characteristics have given it. But we've built a history on that. And for us to go back to our false identities as the basis for our relationship? We're starting on the wrong side and we're ending up at the wrong point. And that's why we're mired in this vicious cycle of chaos.

So, for me, there was some repenting and renouncing that was called for—before we could advance to the stage of developing personal relationships across racial lines. First, there was the matter of the deserted reconciliation program the white guys had initiated because they felt guilty about forsaking minorities at luncheons and statewide prayer movements.

This thing they created that they thought was going to be some mechanism for creating warm and beautiful relationships between blacks and whites had been smashed, and the black community was totally disillusioned by it. But it was God who brought us through that pain and destruction; he showed us there's something much bigger at stake than our pettiness and how we saw this reconciliation movement. Now I believed he was piecing things together, bringing us back together again.

Another black eye that needed attention was the reexamination of the business deal that had gone bad for the African-American entrepreneur and his white backers. After the fallout, the black businessman had reached out

I was often the only African American in a room full of white guys.

to me and some of his black brothers for emotional support. To me, the separation provided an opportunity for atonement—not to resolve the business issue—but to find out if any type of conciliation between blacks and whites was possible following such a breach of faith. Because that's when the real test comes. Hey, when you fail me and disappoint me, how do we get past that? Or do we just fall back into the same old stuff?

After my examination of the business deal gone bad, what I discovered about the failed venture was no big revelation: People in business don't have true relationships. Most don't even care about the other. That business failure was just an extension of our failed relationship. It's got to be about more than white guys giving money to support a black businessman.

That costly incident discouraged many of those who were trying to do something positive in the world of race relations, but the failure actually spawned a new chapter of relationship building. It opened the door to a better understanding of what needed to transpire before any attempts at conciliation could occur. It became clear to all involved that that process could not be bought or paid for. It had to begin with both black and white men facing their failures and owning up to them, as well as taking a hard look at collective failures that had been bred over centuries. As the six of us realigned, we continued to dig deeper to uncover what separated us. What we discovered was not a major surprise—there was a lot of mistrust and hatred.

In the Bible God says you're a liar if you claim to love him but hate your brother. So we failed in our mandate to love God because our loving him is predicated on us showing love and affection for one another. In fact, it's in that failure of our inability to even care about each other that God then emerges as the true reconciler.

Dedicating ourselves to working on personal relationships seemed to resonate with the six men who had committed to the process. What we all discovered within our racial context was no true brotherly love at all. And what was being postured was little more than role-playing. Whether subconscious or not, that role-playing had penetrated everything about who we were—to the point we had become trapped in it—not even able to recognize our own falsehoods. Our only saving grace was we reached that discernment together, understanding we were all stuck with seemingly no way out of the situation. There was only one way to turn, and that was to our Creator.

Surrendering to God—and then submitting one to another—began to create the essence of what friendship looks like. We basically asked God to save us because we had no idea what it looked like to become friends. Or what it meant to love one another.

Once the six of us made it our focus to first be reconciled to our Creator, we began the challenging work of building cross-cultural relationships. We dove into the Scriptures to learn what true reconciliation was supposed to look like. Then we tried to integrate those directives and the words of Jesus into our daily lives.

Soon six became twelve—still half black, half white—as word spread about a group in town lifting up the name of Jesus and exploring real reconciliation in a racist world. Black men from various fellowships in North and Northeast Portland began to hear the positive reports about men reaching across racial divides. At first they didn't come because they didn't believe race relations could ever improve in Portland. But I encouraged them to stop by to see for themselves. Many were intrigued enough they never left.

Like Jeff Moreland, a younger corporate dude I literally ran into during a pickup basketball game. He was a rising star at Chase Manhattan, an up-and-comer who seemingly had a bright future in business. But he shared that selling out to the racist institutionalism of the corporate world forced him to not be himself—he responded one way at his workplace to be socially accepted and differently at home with his wife and family. That pretense led him to a place of deep depression, even to the point of considering suicide. By opening up to the white men he found some peace...and friendship:

"I'm angry at the white guys right now!" he scolded. "You have no idea what I have to deal with cuz of the system I have to operate in that you dominate and control. I have to fight it every day!"

Something amazing happened after that. One of the white guys—who also happened to work in the financial industry—came alongside Jeff and became his mentor. Today those two men are closer than brothers.

With me and Wendell steering, the focus remained on establishing one-on-one relationships between people of different color. The twelve of us meeting together weekly to talk about tearing down the walls that separated us was a big part of the process, but getting out of the small boardroom we were meeting in and into the backyard barbecue scene was where the real relating took place. As in meeting the wife and kids. Breaking bread together. Watching the game. Talking about life and smoking fine cigars late into the evening. One of the white guys who grew up in Eastern Oregon organized hunting trips to his favorite spots in the backwoods. We went to Blazer basketball games. Frequented the local jazz clubs. Some made real estate investments together. One white guy saved a friend from losing his house to foreclosure while he was unemployed. When the group learned one of the black guys and his wife had never taken a honeymoon, an envelope showed up with two round-trip tickets to Maui and a two-week stay at a timeshare. "This is what they do," the grateful recipient would tell people. The men were willing to put more than just their words on the line for their friends.

But it wasn't all fun and games. Even though Wendell and I were kindred spirits, we acknowledged having spirited disputes just like the other blacks and whites. Men were ironing out their differences. And sometimes iron sharpening iron created sparks.

The fact is you're going to have disagreements with anybody you have a relationship with. Because if I love you, then I'm compelled to tell you what I see. Sometimes Wendell and the other white guys didn't want to hear what me and the black men had to say because it was painful.

CHAPTER TWENTY-TWO

Uncomfortable

One of the ancillary attractions to our race-based efforts—but not necessarily for the white guys—was the authority displayed by Larry in conversations, particularly those that elevated to arguments. He was big, bold, and opinionated. He carried his cop presence into meetings and—when he wanted—he had no problem intimidating those in attendance. Plus he was very knowledgeable about the atrocities of the past perpetrated against his ancestors. While the white men remained oblivious, Larry could cite chapter and verse of all the moments in history when black people had been marginalized. And beaten. And raped. And tortured. And lynched. It was hard to argue with him. Because he was right.

Larry gave voice to feelings broadly held in the black community at the time. He was masterful at articulating what other blacks were thinking—but would never say—because they knew if they were ever to express their true feelings about white dominance or white privilege, they would pay a price for it, like losing their job.

Larry's representation of the interests of African Americans endeared him to a lot of younger black men, too. That's because they witnessed him speaking from a position of power to those they viewed as the ruling white evangelical establishment. He also had credibility as a police officer and legitimacy in their eyes as a well-known and active black man in their community. So, in the eyes of the black men, he became kind of a de facto spokesman because he had a pretty good grasp of what the problem was. And then because he was angry and mad and bold—kind of careless—they would defer to him to say what they would have wanted to say. At the same time, that was an alienating factor to others because he was a loud bully scaring everybody.

It would typically be a white man who would be turned off by Larry's boorish behavior and leave, never to return. But I also witnessed the rapt attention and respect black men gave him. It was a distinction I couldn't totally comprehend. All I knew at the time was the tension in those weekly confrontational meetings became magnetic because more and more men were being pulled into the fray.

As long as the truth was being spoken, I was mostly okay with the hostility in the room. The challenge was the black guys' truth-telling was often loud, confrontational, and in-your-face. The white guys were perpetually uncomfortable with the street language, the vocal fights, the turning over of tables and chairs, the threats to "take it outside." And that was mostly between the black guys interacting with each other! Add the Alpha Male complex to the mix and you had the makings for some strong disagreements—no matter your skin color.

My observation was God was sending guys who were willing to press in, men who would say and do whatever it took so others would know the truth. Some might think that's the job of the church—God sends pastors to share the gospel with parishioners. But in America you're not going to find a house of worship half white and half black where the two groups actually care about each other. And there certainly wouldn't be any F-bombing or pew tossing in their efforts to understand one another. The question is, which setting is more real?

Which situation is more relevant to today's spiritual, social, economic, and cultural realities?

I believe we were doing what church was designed for: coming together around the name of Jesus Christ, teaching from the Bible, talking about the gospel, worshiping at times, loving each other, and working on matters of the heart. We were about redemption.

One of the hurdles to overcome in our understanding of each other was the issue of "white privilege." As an example of its insidiousness, one day Larry asked the white men what it meant to be white in America. All he got back were puzzled stares.

"What do you mean?" they asked.

"Well, don't you think it's peculiar that you don't know what it means to be white?" he responded. "You always ask us about the black experience, but you don't know what the white experience is?"

There were some lame attempts, but the answers he got were descriptions of normal human behavior: Being white means I can be a free thinker. The pursuit of happiness. I can work to provide for my family.

The responses confirmed what Larry already knew: white people don't realize being white is not synonymous with being human. The answers described humanity, not anything associated with the "white condition." And the inference was—in their minds—white was normal and everything that wasn't white was somehow abnormal, or in addition to being normal.

"It's amazing to me the extent you white guys don't know yourselves," Larry told us. "It's hilarious, almost. But actually, it's pretty sad because a lot of black people have been influenced and injured by white privilege."

It's a common condition among whites in America—the average white man can't see his white privilege because it's been programmed into him over centuries. And he's oblivious to it. The problem—as I have learned and am certainly guilty of—is out of white men's arrogance and ignorance we have no idea what it's like to walk in the shoes of a black man.

I've seen it for myself: I go into a store with tattered jeans, wild hat, looking like a redneck, and nobody gives me a second look. But when a black guy—with his nice Nike sweats on and cool sunglasses—walks those same aisles, the security guard follows him. There are many doors opened for white people through no virtues of their own—that's white privilege. And conversely, opportunities are denied black people just because of their skin color.

White privilege was a very difficult concept for a lot of the Caucasian men to wrap their heads around. That's because we grew up in a nation where white people wrote the history books. From our education and training, it's easy to assume white people were the baseline medium by which all humanity was judged. We weren't just another cultural group living in a land called America, after all. Whites were the dominant culture, so that made us better than everybody else, right?

Dealing with these kinds of controversial subjects actually fueled our growth and forced us out of the tiny conference room where we had been gathering for about two years. A move also coincided with a different day to meet because Larry's schedule at the police bureau had changed and the group agreed to meet on a Friday—his new day off. From then on we called ourselves "the *Friday* group." We ended up at a much larger space nearby that housed a food bank and counseling center. Turns out the guy who was the recipient of Larry's choke-hold ministry outreach ten years earlier ran the place. We definitely needed the extra room, too, because by then we had opened the sessions to all comers. But although the day and place had changed, the men didn't leave behind their propensity for salting their language with cuss words. Eventually our new landlord gave an ultimatum: No swearing, nothing crude or rude better come out of our mouths. Or else we would have to find another place to meet.

So, for a while, equal numbers of white men and black men would file in every Friday morning, pick their chair in the circle, wait their turn to talk, and share their lives in a mostly orderly fashion. But that didn't last long. Pretty soon some of the black guys started dropping out. It got so one-sided sometimes the split would be a dozen white guys and only one or two African Americans. We asked Larry why. He was blunt:

"You run 'em off! Because the format you created excludes them. You want to compel them to capitulate to the way you communicate, but black folks don't sit there and raise their hand to speak and wait for someone else to finish. We never talk like that. When we communicate, it's always controlled chaos, but it's not disrespectful."

The black guys had been driven away because they couldn't tolerate our white-orchestrated group dynamic with its program routines and new rules of behavior. If they couldn't be themselves establishing real relationships, what was the point? Larry was applying pressure to both sides. He was twisting the arms of his black compatriots to live out their God-given mandate to love one another outside of the church (that place of separation evidenced by the monochromatic makeup of its Sunday services). And he was enlightening us white men about what reconciling with African Americans would really look like working.

"You can't have a white male–dominated meeting and expect black folks to show up and participate," he told us over and over. "They just ain't going to do it. You think your way of facilitating orderly meetings is good, but for the black guys it's boring and humiliating. That kind of white man's rhetoric creates separation. It turned the black guys off."

How to get back on track? We had asked why the blacks were boycotting the racial reconciliation meetings and we had gotten a response. Now, what were we willing to do at that critical juncture?

We made a radical decision, something that would probably never happen in the white community anywhere else. The black guys would be in charge, and we would be subservient to them. They would take on the leadership role; what they said went.

Easier said than done. With its history of exclusion laws, sundown laws, and redlining real estate practices, Portland, Oregon, had never experienced such a reversal of racial roles. And, with the city's population at the time dominated twelve to one whites over blacks, it seemed impractical a group of white businessmen would consent to such an arrangement. Impractical and probably impossible to sustain, most would say. First of all, men—white, black, brown, red, yellow, or polka dot—have a built-in aversion to being subservient or submissive. And secondly, battles have been waged for centuries in America to ensure the white man maintained his role as the dominant race. Bucking that would be hard to swallow.

Out of our comfort zones. That's where us white guys were heading; or more accurately, were being led by the black men. It was unknown territory to all of the other white men, except for me. I had endured a taste of black leadership years earlier, and I can still honestly say I felt uncomfortable dealing with race relations. But I vowed to stay committed to the process. And to my friendship with Larry.

CHAPTER TWENTY-THREE

The Social Contract

Of course white guys feel totally threatened with blacks owning the majority opinion. That's why they've worked so hard to never let it get to the point where they have to be subject to somebody else's way of communication. They've always been threatened by that because they believe deferring to the black man's way means a lowering of standards. I've heard that for years, and frankly that demonization of the way we communicate is insulting.

So I made a declaration: in order for black leadership to become the voice of the movement—which is what the old white guys said they wanted—any white influence would need to be controlled. I laid down the gauntlet before them: White men, learn to submit yourself to your black brothers. Lay down your control. Take that ownership you think you're entitled to and give it up. I basically summed it all up by telling the white guys to shut their mouths and listen to the black guys.

An interesting phenomenon developed. When the message spread that the movement to improve race relations in Portland had been restructured so blacks were in charge, younger African-American men started showing up. The new faces included several reformed gang members like Bloods Ayric Payton—the kid from Ready Ribs days who got ambushed by a Crip— and Michael Fesser—the Woodlawn play caller who had professed his hatred toward me, as well as his desire to kill me. And what attracted them? It wasn't the other black men—the pastors, the city workers, a couple entrepreneurs, some businessmen—it was the older white men.

I got up in front of the group one *Friday* and there were twenty young African Americans in there! I didn't even realize there were that many younger brothers showing up because I had been so busy yelling at the white guys and beating them up. The young guys came to *Friday* because they were intrigued by what was happening. They wanted to witness the dynamics being worked out between the two groups. It was something they had never seen before. They wanted to hear the exchanges. They wanted to be part of the conversation—especially the dialogue that revealed the privileges the whites enjoyed...at the expense of the black person. What they discovered was the white men remained totally clueless about their white privilege.

It's clearly evident to us that on a daily basis—for those with white skin—obstacles disappear, which clears the way for them to receive special conditions and circumstances...as if they were the white man's birthright. What really pisses off black folks is white people don't even have to be aware of themselves or of how other people respond to them. Because there is no intra-cultural penalty for the white guys not knowing. You can exist totally ignorant of my African-American culture. But for a black man to not know about white culture, there is an inherent penalty in that—and it can have a dire consequence on my livelihood. At *Friday*, where these types of difficult issues were debated, the white men often felt under attack. And because they didn't have a means to comfortably deal with what it meant to be a benefactor of white privilege, they would often retreat into silence.

So, whenever the white guys clammed up or tried to portray themselves differently, I had to call them out. And, of course, Wendell was my favorite scapegoat. More times than I can count, I painted an unflattering picture of him as the embodiment of an arrogant white racist society. I held him up in story after story as the soulless white man who didn't care and wasn't empathetic to the black man's plight. When he tried to push back, I told him he needed to be Wendell—that white bigoted-ass racist dude trying to understand himself. Those young black guys didn't want whites coming over to try to appeal to them, they needed to engage whiteness from a black perspective.

And I made it very clear whenever I led discussions about race white people would always be uncomfortable. Because what's happening between blacks and whites in America has little to do with racism or "racial reconciliation." It's all about mitigating whites' comfort levels. So, if the men of *Friday* want to get serious about getting to the point of reconciliation, what I got to do is take you out of your comfort zone and put you in the black man's world.

But the problem was the black man's world was foreign to ninety-five percent of Portlanders...because they were white. Maybe some had read a little about African-American history in school. Others might have moved to Portland from somewhere like Chicago or Atlanta where they experienced the black condition. A few, like Wendell, probably watched the black man's story unfold on TV's evening news during the volatile fifties and sixties. But for most there was only an obliviousness to the underlying current that flowed from the era of slavery, segregation, civil rights, and race riots. Yes, those were real episodes in American history that have undoubtedly infiltrated the minds and hearts of white people. But somehow—even though the indelible markings of prejudice are prevalent—white people seem unaware of their racist tendencies today.

And we—black folks—have effectively been removed from the white person's consciousness, except to the extent you see us. That's why Wendell couldn't see who I was when I came to his office with Cliff Robinson. He never saw me as a father, husband, gentleman, responsible member of my community. He only saw my outrage at a system that has villainized my color, vilified my culture, and put the face of poverty on me. He just chalked it up to me being an angry black man. And when I don't fit into that category, somehow white people try to put me there.

It may not be signed and dated, but I've come to believe there exists deep in the recesses of the white person's brain a document of understanding that dictates how they act towards people of color. There's even a term for it—the Social Contract Between Whites and Blacks. Or as others have defined it, White Supremacy.

Even my own father, who had grown up at a time when white men beat black men just because they could, had tried to instill in me as a youngster how I needed to act around white people: Don't look them in the eye. Don't talk unless they speak to you first. Say "Yes, sir," and "No, sir." I rebuffed the teaching of that shameful behavior, but I came to understand my dad was just trying to protect me.

I felt like an enigma who was catching hell from both sides. As a young black man, I had joined an almost all-white police force that shunned me. And as a cop, I patrolled mostly all-black neighborhoods and put hundreds of black men behind bars. One side said I was incompetent, unwanted, a failure. The other called me a traitor, a sell-out, an Uncle Tom.

I used to think I had these big shoulders so I could beat the crap out of everybody else. But God told me, "You got those shoulders because you can take a beating." For most of my career with the Portland Police Bureau, I defied that invisible contract that expected me to "know my place" as a black man in the white man's world. I never acted like the subservient black guy; I didn't play political games to get promoted. I was always respectful of those in positions of authority, but I commanded respect in return. When that mutual respect eroded with the arrival of a new police chief, I knew it was time to go.

I had stayed on as minority recruiter much longer than the one year I had promised my wife—I actually spent eight years in Personnel—and I may have worked longer if not for the rude ten-day notice that I was to be transferred back to operations...as a uniformed patrol officer. The reason for the sudden transfer? "Wanted to head in a different direction," was the word out of the police chief's office.

Sure, I acknowledge I was very vocal about things inside and outside the bureau at the time. But I believe the move was the bureau's final attempt at trying to shut me up. They weren't about to fire their African-American minority recruiter—that would look bad. And besides, I hadn't done anything egregious to warrant termination. So they essentially pushed me out the door of administration and told me to put my walking shoes back on.

There wasn't so much as a "Thank you for all your hard work." Basically, "Just get out and shut your mouth about it." Apparently they wanted someone more docile, but that ain't me. So I resigned. But to add injury to insult, the week after my resignation the stock market crashed. With it went about a third of my savings. It took me a long time to get over the humiliation of that transfer and the devastation of my bank account. The bureau tried to add further disgrace by arguing I technically had worked for the police depart-

Being relegated to street cop after an eight-year stint in Personnel expedited my retirement from the force.

ment twenty-seven years—not twenty-eight—because my first year of work, they said, was as a civilian in the law enforcement training program.

Evidence the so-called Social Contract Between Whites and Blacks is still alive and kicking? Proof that whites take their supremacy seriously, at the expense of blacks?

We can't pretend these constructs don't exist. I believe the cultural explanation—what we've been taught it means to be black and what we've been taught it means to be white—is a design to divide us and keep us separated. So, if I define myself as a black person and you as a white person, we are never meant to be together.

It literally torments me to be aware of who white people are and, subsequently, the circumstances we as blacks are subject to. In fact, it's torture to me. White people think nothing about race when a fellow Caucasian does something spectacular or incredibly stupid. But when a black person does something spectacular or incredibly stupid, whites either consider them a credit to their race or a discredit to all the other black people.

For example, when O.J. Simpson walks out of court a free man after being acquitted of murdering his ex-wife, he is a discredit to his entire race. But when convicted murderer Jeffrey Dahmer kills and eats people, well, that's just one depraved guy acting on his own; doesn't have anything to do with all the other white people.

The double standard runs deep. And it hurts. Personally, there is no benefit to me for being the stick that stirs up all these hard feelings about race relations. Only pain. A pain I live with every day.

CHAPTER TWENTY-FOUR

He Goes Where You Don't Want To

Larry paid a price—both personally and professionally—for being a good cop. The social contract dictates that for a black man to succeed in a white world, he needs to be friendly, docile, cheerful, helpful, courteous, and kind. Well, Larry violated that contract every day at work. And he also caught a lot of heat from those in African-American neighborhoods who judged he had violated their trust and sold out to the white man. I've been around the man long enough to witness the various forms of discrimination dumped on him daily. Larry persevered at the police department as a black man who regularly dealt with the inequities foisted upon him at his institutional workplace. But he never kowtowed to the white establishment. And he didn't abide by the rules of the social contract, which probably cost him his career.

The social contract language the black guys introduced us to sorely convicted many of the white men—once there was acknowledgement of its underpinning that "whites are superior and right, while blacks are inferior and wrong." But it wasn't easy for white men to get to that point of discernment. We couldn't see our own indifference. We were blind to the contract's unspoken traits that shaped how we perceive the black man's world. So, it was up to our black friends to point out what we didn't know about ourselves.

And for some reason, Larry always seemed to be the one at the front of that line. He was relentless, but I believe him when he says he takes no joy in the knowledge he has gained and his understanding of the white man's world.

Some say Larry is gifted, an insightful communicator who listens to the spirit of God and responds by pressing in to men's lives to uncover areas where transformation and healing are needed. Others counter there's no gifting related to an obnoxious boor calling out someone's flaws in public, especially by a person they don't know or trust. But all can agree there's a fine line between speaking the truth into someone's life...and doing so out of love. You can't have one and not the other in the reconciliation process. The key, according to the apostle Paul, is to speak the truth in love because that was Christ's example. First-time visitors to the *Friday* experience might not understand the Love part when the brutal Truth is going on, but if they hang in long enough they usually get the picture.

I tend to agree with Larry's best friend, Greg Taylor, who says Larry is misunderstood by a lot of people who don't know him. "If you look real close, you can see he really loves people, I mean, a lot—enough to take on all the repercussions for doing what he believes he needs to do in order to help people," Greg told me. "Because it's hard. Just think if you were the big jerk in a meeting who always had to point out every-body's faults and somehow get them to see it themselves. Imagine all the misunderstandings that can go along with that."

Greg, a supervisor at one of Portland's wastewater treatment facil-ities, likens what Larry does to his crew's motto: *We go where you don't want to.* That's what Larry does. He goes where you don't want to.

Trying to reconcile your differences with another human being is a messy business. It is hard work; full of conflict. The process can be painful, like treating a crusty scab that keeps getting ripped off...over and over without mending. It can also be beautiful and transformational. Those who stay the course will be changed—some from their short-term involvement, others from a life-long dedication to resolving differences between people.

Thousands of men who have been touched by *Friday* have experienced varying degrees of reconciliatory change in their own lives. And the ripple effects of these powerful transformations have positively affected untold others in their spheres of influence—families, communities, and even extending nationally and internationally. Some men's lives were touched after a single exposure to a *Friday* event, friendship, or testimony. Others breezed through a couple of *Fridays* and never came back—either not ready, not interested, or not compatible with its foundations in the Scriptures. Larry and I have been involved from the start—dedicating more than two decades of our lives to building relationships across racial lines. And a core group making up the *Friday* faithful has invested years in the relational effort.

Of course, not everyone is attracted to sorting out their feelings about race relations, but *Friday* is more about relations than it is about race. As one of the African-American guys described it, "If you dangle the carrot, the horse will follow. God, instead of dangling a carrot, he uses 'racial reconciliation' to draw men in." *Friday* is—first and foremost—about reconciling with our Creator. Its second calling is the biblical reference to be in relationship with our neighbors, the people with whom we come into contact. That mission just happens to involve people of all races, religions, and cultures.

The model is built on relationships, best exemplified when men are honest about their needs and transparently offer themselves up to be heard by God and the men of *Friday*. Complete surrender. Authentic confession. Total submission. Absolute forgiveness. That's the ideal. It's also very difficult for a man—with his ego, his title, his fears—to actually be real and want to reveal himself to other men. Confuse that with religiosity and the challenge of intimacy is compounded. Heap on the raw street language— what some call unadulterated grown-men conversation—and going public with your transgressions can be downright intimidating.

When it comes to putting one's life on display, some men are more comfortable than others sharing their innermost thoughts, desires, and shortcomings. They may be reluctant to open up for a variety of reasons: Their trust might have been betrayed in the past. They're fearful about potential repercussions ("People won't like me if they knew who I really was."). They might be too embarrassed or ashamed of what they've done.

Then there are others whose lives are like an open book. They're comfortable in their thin skin. They invite you to walk in their shoes, to ask anything, to talk about everything. They thrive on transparency. Those are the rare ones.

And then there are those individuals who possess shades of both characteristics, and—to them—how open or closed they become depends on the person on the other side of the conversation. They're often high achievers, strong-willed, bold, fighters. They are the last men standing. But if you're used to being the last one standing, you're definitely used to being in charge, in control. You're the Alpha Male. But what happens when there's another Alpha Male right across from you? It can be dangerous when there's more than one around.

During our three-year run at Reflections—a meeting space connected to the police bureau's North Precinct where we moved after getting kicked out of the food bank—*Friday* attracted some really big hitters. These weren't the kind of men you'd find on the baseball diamond or on Wall Street, but everyday warriors and scrappers who wouldn't back down from a fight. The back room of the restaurant was starting to look like a boxing ring with both vocal and physical altercations, as well as a few veiled threats to continue the "conversation" outside. Fortunately, its location next to the police precinct prevented any escalation of boisterous disagreements. Of course, smack dab in the middle of those skirmishes one would find the loud, large, and brash personality known as Larry Anderson. I would often get swept up in the melees, too, and with all of my 170 pounds I tried to be the peacekeeper.

One of the guys who bounced in and out of *Friday* went toe-to-toe with Larry in a heated exchange his first time in front of the group. The big guy apparently had something he wanted to get off his chest, and when he raised his hand to speak, Larry shut him down. Actually shouted him down with a "Shut the fuck up and sit down!" The guy's protests to have his voice heard were rebuffed...and he subsequently simmered there in silence the rest of the meeting. Afterwards, he came up to Larry, not to yell at him or start a fight for the perceived slight, but to thank him. I didn't discover what that was all about until later when the guy told me his story. To the best of my recollection, here is what he said:

> While it's not the kind of men's group for me—I do meet regularly with some other fellow believers—I actually benefited greatly from the experience. It certainly wasn't pleasant being yelled at as a first-time visitor and told I couldn't speak my peace, but after much reflection I'm glad my personal agenda got thwarted by Mr. Anderson.
>
> You see, I went to that meeting with a specific reason: it was my selfish intention to seek a blanket absolution from the assembled African-American men for my past racist behavior. I had heard about this weekly forum where

men of different skin colors got together weekly to share their lives. Perfect, I remember thinking, I've harbored a measure of guilt in my life for my bigoted ways, and I figured this would be the ideal time and place to unload my burden. My plan was to introduce myself to the group, admit my past transgressions against the black race, accept their forgiveness, and then go about my business. Neat, tidy, liberating. I'd be fully exonerated by revealing my dirty little secret! Maybe even commended for my brutal honesty. Redeemed by my confession, I would then be freed up to gain their trust and delve into their messy life stories. But it didn't quite work out that way. My pride and my agenda couldn't fit through *Friday's* "No Bullshit Zone," and my attempt at a free pass was stymied.

As I stewed there in my seat for the next few hours, a slow realization came over me. The type of "racial reconciliation" I thought I was there for was fake. These men were authentic. They were real. And their words backed up their convictions. They were all about relationship and truth. If I had been allowed to talk, I would have been skewered for my pretense. I might as well have put a sign on my forehead that declared who I was—a phony who wanted the easy way out. So that's why I thanked Larry Anderson. I don't know if he realized it, but that morning he saved me from myself.

After that day, this notion of real reconciliation continued to prick my conscience. I thought about the harm done to others either purposely or out of my ignorance. Of damaged relationships that needed repair. Of people I had wronged and never made amends. Here I was, willing to reconcile with complete strangers, but what I realized from my *Friday* intervention was there were people in my life, important people, who I had hurt and had never owned up to the pain I caused them.

You and your brotherhood had a major impact on me. I've since restored relations with certain family members and others I have wronged. And I don't believe I would have had the clarity and the courage to reconcile those relationships without my uncomfortable but rewarding short-time experience at your *Friday* group.

I can honestly say I have struggled over the years whenever I have tried to gauge the success of our *Friday* endeavors. Men come and go. Some stay, but the majority move on after a while. I get encouraged when I hear stories recounting positive personal experiences from a brief encounter. And I'm left with questions when a guy shows up only once and we never hear from him again. Like the time the naïve Pillsbury Dough Boy showed up:

Larry (kicking off a *Friday* session with about thirty men in the room): "Anybody got something to confess that we need to deal with?"

New white guy—pudgy, red hair, with hand raised: "Yeah, I do."

Larry: "What's your name? What? Can't hear you...I'm going to call you Pillsbury Dough Boy. What you got to confess?"

Dough Boy (early thirties): "I don't get along with my dad."

Larry: "What you mean, you don't get along with your dad?"

Dough Boy: "He was mean to my mom and me, and then he left us."

Larry: "Explain 'mean.'"

Dough Boy: "He hit my mom."

Larry: "And what did you do about it?"

Dough Boy: "I was only five."

Larry: "Your dad beat your mom and you didn't do anything about it?"

Dough Boy (stymied, confused): "Huh?"

Larry: "So how do you feel about your dad now?"

Dough Boy: "I don't like him."

Larry: "What do you mean, you don't like him?"

Dough Boy: "I'm mad about it, angry."

Larry: "And you don't talk to your dad? No relationship?"

Dough Boy: "No."

Larry: "Do you know what the Bible says about how we should treat our parents?"

Dough Boy: "Yeah, it's one of the Ten Commandments: Honor your father and mother."

Larry: "So God says you're supposed to love and honor your father."

Dough Boy: "But he…"

Larry (getting louder): "Do you love your father?"

Dough Boy (through tears): "After what he did to us?"

Larry (sternly): "Yes, tell me...how you feel...right now...about your dad."

Dough Boy (screaming): "I HATE HIM!! I HATE MY DAD!!!"

Larry: "Okay, now we're getting somewhere. I want you to get on your knees, right in the middle of this circle of men, and ask for God's forgiveness. Now is the time for healing."

As the young man got on his knees and then lay prostrate on the floor, bawling his eyes out, Larry calmly asked the brothers seated around to come lay hands on him. And pray over him. Several minutes went by before the prayer warriors returned to their seats. And the pudgy, red-headed white kid with his face to the floor continued weeping. Healed or humiliated? No one will ever know. Dough Boy never came back to *Friday*.

CHAPTER TWENTY-FIVE

Evangelizing in a Brothel?

First time somebody gets cussed out they wonder what kind of religious group we are. Well, we're not. *Friday* is about what God is doing in our hearts daily. How he's restructured our lives. How he has taken us from our brokenness and brought us into wholeness. He is remaking us into the image of his Son and fitting us together as a body.

Friday isn't an Alcoholics Anonymous twelve-step program. You don't go there to have somebody solve your problems. There is no group therapy, no psychiatrist on staff. There's also no Miranda rights. This is *Friday*'s position: You have the right to shut up, but if you do decide to talk, anything you say can and will be used against you. We just ask, "Man, what you got to say?" And then, when we get you to run your mouth and you start talking about yourself, it takes us about ten minutes to realize everything we need to know about you because God has given us ears to hear and eyes to see. And even if you try to disguise your voice, we hear you loud and clear, and we will take whatever you say and bring it right back to you. It works every time. That's how we know it's God. Now, it may take some dancing and some fighting and some pulling and some breaking down, but eventually it works because God says his Word will never come back empty. It will accomplish what he desires. So when we speak God's word, it opens men's hearts, it lays bare their soul. That's what it will do to you. And that's why people are so uncomfortable with the process.

Our job is to just kick men back into play, because we want to hide behind all kinds of things. We hide in our professions; we hide behind our skin color. The deal is to find out where you're hiding, rip those things down, and throw you in the arena. You might get beat up a little bit and want to run, but we try to keep you in the game.

Keeping men in play became my mission. I got to be pretty good at it at work as the minister-in-training who counseled with and advised officers about their careers. But now that I was retired, a new world of opportunities to share my faith and represent my African-American culture opened up for me. In my personal dealings with people, there was no governor to limit sharing what was really on my heart. Wendell, with his courtroom background and calm demeanor, used a softer approach. He relied on probing questions and encouraging responses to get men to open up and talk about themselves.

But I was much more direct. And while my confrontational style might have turned some off, there were others who welcomed my bold approach. Like the president of the Republic of Benin whom some of us had met at the National Prayer Breakfast. Mathieu Kérékou wanted help spreading the message of reconciliation to his people who had suffered for decades from ethnic strife, riots, and revolts. And he apparently felt the gospel of basketball was the best way to reach his country's young men with the good news of Jesus. So I got to go to Africa as part of an invited group to train and mentor them in the fundamentals of basketball.

But as much as I enjoyed sharing stories about my faith and playing ball with the boys, what I learned about my African ancestry proved sobering and life-changing. I had the opportunity to learn firsthand about the evils of slavery that Benin and its port town of Ouidah had been involved in for more than 200 years. The area had earned the ugly term, "Slave Coast," because an estimated two to three million African slaves had been shipped from there. Other West African coastal regions—such as the Gold Coast, the Ivory Coast, and the Pepper Coast—were also known for their prime colonial exports, but Ouidah, with its shameful past as the epicenter of the slave trade, was an even darker region because of a culture steeped in voodoo religion.

It was a scary place—I could actually feel the oppression around me. It's where the slave traders brought and held captive the hundreds of thousands of men, women, and children they had kidnapped. I walked where they walked. I saw the chains and the stockades. I stooped to peer into the remains of rooms where men, women, and children had been locked up—structures with no windows so as to acclimate the people who were eventually crammed into the holds of ships bound for the Americas. I heard the stories about a supposedly magical tree called the Tree of Forgetfulness, which the captives were forced to circle. Performing that ritual brought on a voodoo curse designed to make them forget their identity, everything about the life they were about to leave behind. And I walked through the Gateway of No Return, represented by a monument at the edge of the sea. The archway is etched with depictions of naked chained men disappearing into the unknown.

For some reason I felt anchored to the continent. On the other hand, I recognized as an African American just how disconnected I really was. I felt drawn to the birthplace of my ancestors, as if I was taking the first step to reconciling with my unknown past. At the same time, I was repulsed by the sense of terror and presence of evil spirits that hung over the land like a dark cloud.

Captured and sold out by your own people. Then told to forget who you are, who your relatives are. And finally—never come back. For hundreds of thousands of Africans, those were the insults that ruined their lives. And affected the lives of millions of others born into that story.

President Kérékou's plea for atonement resonated with me because the leader of Benin was extolling his fellow countrymen to forgive—not forget—the atrocities perpetrated one to another. He implored them to reconcile with each other. Otherwise, he feared, there would be no healing in Africa. I believe we're in the same boat—unless we reconcile with each other, there will be no healing in America.

I shed tears of sadness over the unspeakable acts of betrayal carried out by my ancestors in that place. But I also found hope…in the most unlikely place.

Yes, the trip was intended to develop a basketball program in support of a friend who happened to be the president of his country. But, for me, the Benin trip was never about basketball. Some organizations send workers overseas to dig wells, build latrines, and construct school buildings—and that's all well and good—but, for me, it wasn't about bricks and mortar.

The real work is to establish and maintain relationships. Everything centers on relationships—they are through people, by people, for people, in people. We went over there to teach basketball because that was the medium we were most familiar with, but it was never about basketball. And it never is about basketball.

It's strange, but the strongest relationships I formed on my two trips to Benin were about as far removed from teaching basketball skills to young men as can be imagined. After one especially long day running up and down the courts, a couple of the younger mentors petitioned me to take them out for a drink. I agreed, but I had to ask around because I didn't know the location of the nearest bar. So one of the locals directed us to an establishment on the outskirts of town. It was late when we got to the nightclub, and we were surprised to see more women—beautiful women—than men. Apparently, we soon learned, Beninese don't have "regular" bars like they do in America. They have brothels.

Now I realize most people of faith would frown on a group of men frequenting a place of ill repute, but for some reason I felt compelled to stay. Of course, sitting around the table and being served by certain working women caused my guys who looked up to me to shoot puzzled and disapproving glances my way. I even remember lifting up a prayerful query questioning God's motive in leading me and my fellow followers of Jesus to a brothel. The conversation in my head went something like:

Me: God, is it a mistake we're here?

God: Larry, do you see those women?

Me: Of course, Lord, but I'm embarrassed to be here.

God: Look at those women.

Me: I don't want to look at the women (but I obeyed).

God: Do you see their desperation?

I did. I saw it in their faces. The brokenness. The hopelessness. The despair. At that moment my heart was broken for those women. Looking through God's eyes, I didn't focus on their looks, their dress, or their activities. They were children of God. Others might rain down judgments on them as whores in a brothel. But my vision was illuminated as I saw them as God sees them—his precious daughters.

The guys couldn't believe it when the next night I rounded them up and told them we were going back to the brothel. They were aghast, but I told them there was some unfinished business that needed to be taken care of there. I explained that the previous evening when I got back to the hotel I had begun to second-guess my role in God's plan. They're just a bunch of prostitutes, I told myself as my faith wavered. And I questioned my godly leadership for taking my men into a den of iniquity. But God overcame my doubts and fears, and replaced them with a sense of duty:

"Those are desperate women, who for whatever reason have ended up here. You go be something different to them than they usually get. Because who else is going to come? Who else am I going to send if not you?"

When we arrived the second night, I asked the guys to pool all their money and pick out a couple of girls. Again, they must have thought I had lost my mind—or at least my commitment to my marriage vows. But after paying them their going rates, we invited the young women to sit down and join us at the table. For the rest of the evening we all hung out, talked, and laughed. We did the same the next night. And the night after. It was a strange spectacle—the opposite of what was expected inside a brothel. There were upwards of a dozen women seated around the tables, all not having sex with us five paying customers.

There was lots of laughter and tears, but not a shortage of condemning stares from the rest of the clientele. One of the young girls started crying when she shared the camaraderie with us reminded her of similar moments she had had with her dad before he was killed in the war. Other stories of difficult childhoods and dangerous circumstances brought everyone to tears.

On our last night I announced I had something to tell them. It was a message I believed God wanted me to deliver to the women around the table. First, I told them about the two long plane rides it took to get to Benin—how uncomfortable the tiny coach seats were, how I had been complaining about everything, and asking myself why I even made the trip.

"But now I know why God had me fly all that way," I shared. "For you."

The room went quiet, except for the one young woman who wondered aloud if we were going to marry them and take them home with us. And I was almost in tears as the full realization of why I was in a brothel in Africa overwhelmed me.

"I just want you to know God hasn't forgotten you," I said, fighting back the emotion. "He remembers you. And he wants you to know that he remembers you. He remembers that time with your dad. He remembers those times when you girls sat around laughing and having fun with your families. He knows who you are. And he loves you. He sent us over here to remind you of that."

What a sight: five Christian men from Portland, Oregon, and fifteen ladies of the night in a brothel in Western Africa. All hugging, crying, and

conversing as if we were best friends. There was no Bible thumping, no rec-
itations of the Ten Commandments, no accusatory finger pointing. There
was only love, displayed by a handful of reconcilers—authentic men of God
acting like Jesus would.

When I returned to Benin a year later for the final basketball-themed
mission, I made a point of stopping by the brothel. As soon as I stepped
inside, one of the girls recognized me and shouted, "You came back!" When
she ran over to embrace me, she happily explained that two of the young
women from the previous year had left the brothel. And that she and a
friend were also trying to get out as well. I told her she didn't have to explain
herself; I was just glad to see she was okay.

It's a complicated thing God taught me about how we intrude upon
other cultures with our sense of morality. What happens is we end up
destroying people. We make their lives more miserable because we force our
morality on their situation, which only causes them to be unable to function
where they live.

After I left Africa, I reflected on how God had orchestrated the entire
episode at the brothel—even more than that, how God had orchestrated my
entire life. I had excelled at basketball in school, but never imagined those
skills would transfer to putting on a basketball clinic in Africa. I had studied
God's word at Brother Mac's Open Book Bible Study, but never envisioned
sharing a word from God in a Beninese brothel. I was a leader of men who
were dedicated to resolving their differences, but never in a million years
could I see myself being invited by a president to participate in a reconciliation campaign in a country of nearly ten million. As a policeman—a career I
never thought I would have—I was paid to go into places where prostitutes
hung out. I marveled at how God had considered all the gifts and training I'd
already had and applied them in places like a whorehouse enveloped by evil
spirits and voodoo curses.

Back in Portland, several men who had heard the stories about "just hanging out" with a host of beautiful women in the brothel business remarked to me they could never imagine pulling off something like that themselves.

"Then you ain't ready, partner," I told them. "You ain't God's dude. You disqualify yourself."

I explained to them if God hadn't revealed himself to me in those quiet moments of prayerful reflection, I wouldn't have been able to do it either. Because the flesh is weak. But I would never give up my intimate relationship with God for a moment of pleasure. This is why I am here, and I don't ever want to mess that up.

I told the guys the only way I could evangelize in a brothel is because I had completely surrendered myself to God. I had offered up my morality, my righteous indignation—and God defeated all of it. He humbled me to the point where I was not above that place, those girls, their situation. He wanted me to know that when he sets me before the power seats and the board rooms, when he puts me in front of the presidents and the kings and the queens in the palace, they are just as destitute as those prostitutes. They are just as lonely. They are just as lost.

Sometimes it's the privileged—the ones with the money, the powerful positions, those who look like they've got everything figured out—who are overlooked and not ministered to like the down-and-out. It's easier to see the needs of the poor, the dirty, and the hungry. But the person in high standing—the one who smells good, looks good—he's just as in need of a Savior as the girl down there working in the brothel. In fact, she might be in better shape because she has no problem understanding her situation.

Now, I realize talk of me evangelizing in an African brothel created a stir in some religious circles. A couple years earlier I probably would have tracked those gossipers down and picked a fight with them. Because back then I was full of doubt. And my immaturity had caused me to become combative in my attempts to justify my actions and words. But my defensiveness only caused others to question my authority. Finally, I learned to quit trying to make myself relevant to everyone and just do what I believed God was asking me to do…and not worry about the outcome.

At *Friday* I've gotten to the point where I don't care what people think about me, how I behave, what happens there. Because I care more about you and your relationship than what you think about me and the role I have to play. And besides, most of the white men who come to *Friday* say God told them to go. So I figure God must have had a reason to send them. It was my job to facilitate that discovery. Just like decades earlier when God sent me to Brother McDonald so I could study the Scriptures under his tutelage.

God doesn't say, "Go submit to an organization, a governing body." He says, "Go submit to people." For me, it wasn't, "Go down to Open Book Bible"; it was, "Go down there and submit to Brother McDonald," who's a big jerk, who's in the John Birch Society—*What black man is in the John Birch Society?*—who's a Republican, who's got me in the little John Birch club. I understand submission.

I was submitted to Brother Mac and his training for fifteen years. And I hated it. I couldn't know that—years later—because of that experience, I would come to understand the importance of submission.

So I know firsthand what these white dudes really mean when they tell me, "God told me to come to *Friday*." No, what God is telling you is, "You go down there and submit yourself to that loudmouth black dude that's so offensive to you."

It's in the action of submitting that the real work of *Friday* gets done. When an issue is brought to the surface—and the person is willing to be transparent and vulnerable—transformation can take place. In a sense, the men of *Friday* serve as facilitators. We listen, we ask questions, we provide instruction, and we celebrate victories. We don't waste time dwelling on the problem. We don't need to hear the details of someone's confession he was looking at pornography the previous night while his wife was sleeping. We're not like AA where you focus on your problem and try to improve your behavior.

We acknowledge problems, but we don't fixate on them. If you need therapy or a psychiatrist, go pay for that. We focus on the root of the issue by talking about what God has to say about it. We don't need to be reaffirming all that stuff's in there. What we need to be doing is putting something else in there that defeats it, which is God's word.

CHAPTER TWENTY-SIX

A Different Perspective

When Reflections lost its lease, *Friday* was on the move again. For more than ten years, hundreds of men—almost exclusively Caucasians and African Americans—had passed through *Friday*'s door to hash out a shared vision of racial reconciliation. That's more than 500 face-to-face confrontations between mostly ignorant white guys and mostly angry black men. Of course, our so-called racial reconciliation was—and still is—a journey, more than a destination. But *Friday* slightly changed course when several of the "old guard" white guys dropped out. A few retired, some stepped away completely, and a couple splintered off to form their own group.

Larry was three years into his new "career" as full-time head of the *Friday* movement, and even though I was still defending clients in court, I was done with murder cases. My last one had been so emotionally draining, it kind of propelled me into retirement mode: I had been asked to represent a local pastor's son who had unwittingly shot and killed his dad during a heated argument at their home. Both Larry and I remained committed to Portland's cultural awareness effort, but interestingly, a new dynamic—neither white nor black—helped steer the group in another direction.

When *Friday* reignited at a new location—a youth opportunity school in North Portland—the doors would open at seven a.m. and men from all walks of life would pull up a chair and spend the next several hours wrangling with their different perspectives on important issues of the day. In the mix were business executives, former gang members, attorneys, policemen, ex-cons, preachers, teachers, retirees, students, government workers, and "tourists," a term the group used to describe those who only showed up once or twice.

We typically would have deep discussions centered on race, faith, and family, but no subject—except maybe politics—was off limits. The only mandate was "real" talk. When a man entered that room on *Friday*, it was widely accepted he had crossed through the "No Bullshit Zone." If anything phony or fake was postured, it was called out—and possibly accompanied by an expletive for emphasis. But if you wanted real conversation about real life issues, *Friday* was your platform. Even though there was no agenda and no structure to the sessions, the bottom line was men were there to develop relationships and begin to understand what it meant for blacks and whites—as well as Native Americans, Hispanics, Asians, and others who participated over the years—to live in community. Open dialogue designed to bring harmony out of discord was encouraged. Over the years, books that had been recommended were read and discussed. One in particular that generated a lot of debate was *The Shack*, by author William Paul Young, who was part of *Friday* for many years. And the Bible was always at hand for reading and reference.

The only stipulation—and it was a big one—was no white man could be in charge. The black guys led, everyone else followed. That applied to the content, as well as the way it was communicated. Why? Because white people have disqualified ourselves from leading any form of reconciliation due to our lack of credibility among other cultural groups. Some of the "old guard" had fought to reclaim their credibility, but it proved to be an uphill battle littered with too many unintended painful consequences.

Of course, it hasn't been solely African Americans who have been devastated by the efforts of the white man to change them. Just ask any Native American. *Friday* was blessed at a crucial time in its history to have men representing the First Nations people intersect with the group (some prefer "First Nations" because it captures the essence of their biblical identity as a people created in the image of God, not in the image of European culture). Their life experiences opened our eyes to a whole new dimension of "racial reconciliation."

When Dr. Richard Twiss and Rev. Dr. Randy Woodley showed up at *Friday*, they were probably the most educated and smartest men in the room—any room. And things got explosive when their world collided with the black man's world and the white man's world. Richard earned his reputation as a revolutionary for participating as an eighteen-year-old in a week-long protest inside a federal building that housed the Bureau of Indian Affairs. And Randy shared how his family had been on the receiving end of pure evil intimidation in Kentucky when a white supremacist regularly fired his fifty-caliber machine gun at the corner of their adjoining properties in a successful effort to drive them out of the state.

"You can only imagine what a healing it was for me to be able to sit down with these men in Portland and talk about race," Randy told me. "There's nothing else like *Friday*. You can't find people being that honest anywhere else."

Randy, who teaches at a Christian college, taught us that prejudice and bigotry in this country have been pervasive for centuries, dating back to 1790 when the granting of citizenship was limited to immigrants who were free white persons of good character, thus excluding Native Americans and blacks.

Along with the change in complexion around the proverbial *Friday* table came new perspectives about white privilege, racism, and "racial reconciliation." Richard and Randy—representing their Native American culture—were able to point things out that otherwise would have gotten lost in the duality of whiteness and blackness. One revelation that added clarity to the challenge of relationship-building among races was Richard's sharing that Native people harbored longstanding distrust and anger toward the African-American community. Many western tribes—having no historical frame of reference to place blacks as descendants of Africa—saw them as a different kind of white man. For many Natives, the first black men they saw were the Buffalo Soldiers who fought alongside the U.S. Cavalry. They called them "the Black White men."

And if any of the black guys in *Friday* ever resorted to wallowing in their victimhood by blaming their exclusive brand of slavery for their modern-day struggles, Richard would remind them that—contrary to popular belief—the European colonial practice of importing slaves to North America did not begin with the importation of African tribal people, but with the enslavement of the host people of North America in the 1500s and 1600s. What I really appreciated about Richard was his unwillingness to settle for people's BS. For example, one *Friday* during the Great Recession a white guy commented that unemployment had risen to twelve percent. One of the blacks, known for playing his one-upmanship card, griped that unemployment was at least fifteen percent in the African-American community. Richard, who was listening from across the room—leaning back in his chair in his typical laidback manner—coolly remarked, "Yeahhh, it's ninety percent on the rez." After that there wasn't a lot of parading one's baggage in front of a Native American.

Sometimes it took a different perspective to open the eyes and ears of the assembled black and white men, and I thought Richard was the best at helping paint an alternative picture. Whether for shock value or not, he would say things like, "Until I started hanging out with my black friends, I didn't realize God is black." When I asked what he meant, he said he understood who God is a little better through his black friends' eyes and hearts.

"Before, I just heard yelling, screaming, and anger; now I hear God in the black voice, a voice I understand," he told me. "God is just as black as he is white or Indian or anything else. I've been given who God is to white folks all my life, so now I can say God is black."

The Native culture would look at that as heresy, but Richard was committed to bringing Native-American and African-American worlds together in a way that hadn't been done before. Provocative or not, Richard's message was insightful. If we truly listen, we can all sense who God is from different perspectives. His eye-opening observations served as a meta-narrative for the collective *Friday* experience: that all of us must regain what the First Nations people never lost—the understanding that our togetherness is more important than our individuality.

Richard Twiss, who was a peer of Larry's and mine, loved his Band of Brothers.
[Photo credit: Jim Standridge]

With their wisdom and inspiration, our Native American brothers catapulted us to new levels of understanding and relevance. I believe it was the unheralded friendship between me, Larry, and Richard that caught people's attention. I know Richard, who was recognized as an international expert on the topic of reconciliation, talked about it a lot. He was traveling extensively to speak at churches, colleges, and universities, promoting a simple message to people of all colors around the world: *Nothing significant will happen in the way of reconciliation without honest, Christ-honoring, and truly loving relationships.*

A black man. A white man. And a brown man. History would say those colors don't mix. But Richard would tell anyone who would listen that God is in the business of making the impossible possible. He often referenced the miracle of *Friday* when he was asked to share his unique Native perspective on reconciliation, spirituality, and community. He talked about it during radio interviews, on television, and before groups like Promise Keepers, Campus Crusade for Christ, and Focus on the Family. The word about *Friday* was spreading.

Even though he traveled a lot, Richard was thrilled the year he was asked to share his message of hope for reconciliation at a Portland Business Christmas Luncheon (an honor previously bestowed upon worldwide evangelist Luis Palau for more than twenty years in a row). When he gave the keynote address, he took the stage clothed in his traditional Native dress, beat a drum, danced, and worshiped God in his First Peoples language. The unusual presentation, which was well received by the 700 or so businessmen and women in attendance, was made more remarkable in that none had ever seen a Native American man spreading the Good News of the Gospel at an event celebrating the birth of Jesus.

Richard was also honored to be invited to speak about reconciliation at a National Prayer Breakfast breakout session. He considered it a bonus that a dozen other men from *Friday* accompanied him on the trip to Washington, DC. Richard became a regular attendee at the internationally renowned event—usually adorned in his Native regalia—but his presence there wasn't popular with everyone.

One year, at the luncheon following the president's prayer breakfast, Richard complained to our table of *Friday* friends he had been disrespected by a group of Natives across the way. They apparently didn't approve of Richard's stance that their traditional Native culture and "the Jesus way" were compatible, and they chose to communicate their displeasure by ignoring Richard and not acknowledging him. The snub—at first—went unaddressed. But when Larry heard about it, he said he could relate because he had faced similar rejection as a "traitor," a black cop patrolling the African-American community in North/Northeast Portland. And he wasn't about to let the slight go unanswered. So Larry grabbed his large friend, Greg, and—with Richard and five others of us in tow—he stormed across the Hilton's International Ballroom, making a beeline to the table of unsuspecting Natives. Along the way we captured the attention of most in the crowd of several thousand.

"Hey, my name is Larry, and I think you know my friend, Richard, here," he bellowed, his dramatic booming voice startling the men at the table, as well as most of those seated nearby. "I understand you're being very rude to my friend, and that is not acceptable! After all the stuff you guys have been through in this country, man, and for everything this event represents here, how can you act that ungodly?!"

Stunned silence from the table. And an eerie hush throughout the ballroom followed Larry and his posse back to their table. The place stayed quiet while our cadre of brown and black and white men settled back into our chairs, awaiting the next Christian message that was about to be delivered from the podium.

Men from Oregon have been attending the National Prayer Breakfast since an Oregonian took over organizing the affair in 1958. And for more than twenty years running, men of *Friday* have represented Oregon at the invitation-only breakfast. In breakout sessions during the two days of meetings surrounding the breakfast, Larry, Richard, and I have led workshops, made presentations, and been key participants in ongoing conversations with national leaders about mending relations between people with different cultural backgrounds and skin colors.

So why the focus on attending the National Prayer Breakfast and hammering on the issue of "racial reconciliation" in the nation's capital? It's an expensive undertaking, and you have to be invited. Most first-timers are guests of their paying host. When I first started attending, there were many dark-skinned international attendees, but few—if any—blacks from America. The prayer breakfast mantra is that it is all about relationships, so how is a black man ever going to get to the National Prayer Breakfast if he is not in a relationship with a white guy who can invite him?

Now, I'm sure I wasn't the first white guy to invite a black man to the prestigious event, but it's been important to me to sponsor my friend, Larry, and also several other black friends over the years. Other white men from *Friday* have done the same. Invariably, Oregon's delegation features more African Americans than any other state.

Our presence at the National Prayer Breakfast has become an integral—though unspoken—part of *Friday*. Where else but at our nation's capital could we make a bigger statement that people of all colors in America deserve to be represented? And where else could we make a bigger impact than with an international movement dedicated to reconciliation among all races? And specifically for the black men of *Friday*, is there a bigger stage from which to hear their voices calling for equality and social justice than at the bastion of modern white imperial society? Probably not.

CHAPTER TWENTY-SEVEN

The Right Choice

Some amazing connections have been made at the National Prayer Breakfast. I was there one year when the king of this country comes up to me and asks, "Are you Larry Anderson? One of our cabinet members from the Congo heard about you, and we would like to invite you to come and speak to us." Then there was this other guy I met at the breakfast, and he invited me to his country in Africa where he was running for president. I'm staying in his house, and we were talking about some of the tough issues he was facing there. All of a sudden he turns to me and asks, "So what would you do?" I couldn't believe he was asking me what I thought about running his country!

But it was an invitation from the White House for a meeting after one particular National Prayer Breakfast that got everyone excited. Me, Wendell, Richard—all the guys from *Friday*—had met kings and queens, members of Congress, governors, and ambassadors every year we went to the prayer breakfast. But this time Richard got a very special invite. Because his work in the area of reconciliation had gained such national attention, he had been summoned to meet with senior members of President Obama's team after the breakfast. *Friday*, it seemed, was on the president's radar.

Richard's viewpoints were being heard at the highest levels on issues like immigration, the healing process between First Nations people, and reconciliation among people of all colors. And he and I were in the process of accepting one another, of truly becoming brothers. So one of the things we had agreed on was we were going to DC together with a shared message. We promised we wouldn't let the powers that be divide our movement and separate us or try to use our individual agendas against one another. We said we were going to come together as brothers. We were going to be together, no matter what.

Richard had arrived at the Washington Hilton a few days before the rest of his Band of Brothers—that's what he called all of us in *Friday*—and when I got there I thought he looked a little sick. But he shrugged it off, chalking it up to a bout of food poisoning.

The day before the breakfast with President Obama we rendezvoused in the hotel lobby, excited to join our Pacific Northwest contingent later that night for dinner with our host Andrew Young—respected civil rights activist, Atlanta mayor, and U.S. ambassador to the United Nations during the Jimmy Carter administration. Ambassador Young has been one of my heroes growing up—and I have had the privilege of spending significant time with him since then—but that night was the first time any of us had met the icon.

I was about ready to head up to my room to change for dinner when I noticed Richard was kind of slouched over in one of the Hilton lobby chairs. When we got to him he acknowledged he wasn't feeling well, and he announced he was going for a walk. His friend, Michael Bishop, who is part Muskogee Indian and part black, insisted on going with Richard.

Michael told me later that as soon as he got Richard outside, the light in his eyes—all his amazing presence—left him. He started throwing up and he had the dry heaves. So Michael turned around and headed back to the hotel. On the way he had a vision, which he shared with me:

> We were standing on the steps outside, right near the area
> where President Reagan was shot. Richard could barely walk,

so he's holding on to me with both arms, taking one step at a time. I'm holding him like he's an invalid at this point. And that's when I had this vision. It was like a portal opened up down by his left leg—a tall rectangular clear window that was kind of hazy around the edges. I saw his foot with his black shoe on it, but above it the leg was only bone from the knee down. It was just like a skeleton, like I was looking at a mirror that reflected a leg with no clothes on it, no meat, just a shoe and white bone. I know, it sounds crazy. It scared the crap out of me.

An omen? Michael was so shaken by the strange manifestation and Richard's deteriorating condition he practically carried him back to the hotel where he was going to call 911. But then an amazing transformation took place.

As soon as he got Richard through the front revolving doors of the Hilton, with everybody looking at us, the craziest thing happens—he straightens right up, walks over to the front desk, and very diplomatically says, "Uh, is there a doctor around? I'm having some bad indigestion and I've been sick for a couple of days."

A doctor was summoned; after a brief examination he declared Richard was probably suffering from indigestion and needed some TUMS® and Gas-X®. Everyone was amazed how much better he looked after he took the medicine. I could hardly believe the turnaround. Half-an-hour before, Richard had been puking his guts out, could barely walk, and looked half-dead. Now, here he was smiling and talking to everybody as if nothing had happened!

After we changed clothes most of us headed downstairs for the dinner. And as we filed into the ballroom I looked back to see Richard coming down the stairs. Looks like the medicine worked, I remember thinking to myself. But I started worrying when our table filled up and there was one empty seat—Richard's. That's when word got to us that Richard had collapsed. One of our group left immediately and volunteered to check in on Richard and keep the rest of us updated with text messages.

The first text came in: "Richard is down."

It was followed shortly with: "He's not breathing."

And then: "Now security is doing CPR on him."

Just as Andrew Young leaned over to ask what was going on, another text arrived: "They've called an ambulance." Mr. Young asked me to keep him posted. Right before he got up to give his speech, I let him know Richard was at the hospital. Mr. Young led off his address with a prayer request: "I just want everybody to know that a good friend of ours, Richard Twiss, has fallen. We don't yet know what has happened, but we need to pray for him."

I was kind of incoherent at that point, checking my phone for messages and trying to pay attention to what Andrew Young was saying. I just remember he gave a moving tribute to Richard and said we should honor what he stood for. And then he goes into this whole thing about regularly losing people when he was in the civil rights movement. And he looked right at me and said, "There's some great work we have to do; you make sure you do the great work." Even though I can't remember all he said, it really moved me. It was almost like a spiritual experience.

After dinner, all of us *Friday* guys reunited at George Washington University Hospital where Richard was being worked on in the Intensive Care Unit. "It didn't look good" was all the doctors would tell us.

While the rest of the men were praying, I purposely sat alone in the corner of the ICU's lobby where I had more of a conversation with God than a prayer. I acknowledged even though it was me and Wendell who had started a so-called racial reconciliation effort in the Pacific Northwest some twenty years earlier, Richard was a peer...and probably the one best suited to represent issues of reconciliation nationally and internationally. He was the one who had been summoned to the nation's capital to sit on various panels. He was the one who traveled the world speaking about reform, equality, and acceptance. Richard was the one with an invitation from the White House in his pocket to meet five p.m. the next day with senior members of President Obama's staff.

And I was okay with all that. I had been the front man of *Friday* for a long time, but it would have been fine by me if Richard were to become the spokesperson going forward. He and I had already established an unspoken language where he knew I felt comfortable around him, so it was easy for me to sit back and let him speak, or for me to come alongside him to take on a certain issue together. It's like being a spearhead—when you're at the tip of the spear, everything is dangerous. I thought, man, if I could defer to Richard sometimes as that spear tip, and just kind of deal with stuff on the side, not taking the brunt, that would be pretty cool. And, in my opinion, he was more than capable of doing that; he was more than willing to do that. In fact, he was already doing that anyway.

As I was sitting there, thinking about Richard, realizing he was gone, and missing my friend, I heard a voice: *"Whatsup bro?"* When I looked around to see who was asking me the question, I realized Richard was the only person who spoke like that around me. That was something he always said to me because he thought it was a black thing. Number one, I don't say, "Whatsup bro," and secondly, I didn't see anybody talking to me. Then I heard, *"Hey, I'll see ya later, but not now."* I think he was telling me he was cool. And he was gone. And it was okay.

When some of the guys came over, they offered to pray for Richard's recovery. But I already knew. "Richard's gone," I told them. "He's gone."

Officially, Richard Twiss passed away three days later—with his wife, Katherine, and four sons at his side. They told her the type of heart attack Richard had was the one they call the widow maker, and only a small percentage of people survive that. He had been unconscious since the heart attack and died after they removed life support.

His untimely death was devastating to his family, friends, co-workers, students, and his *Friday* Band of Brothers. Our only consolation was we knew Richard was with the Creator he loved, and we would someday all be reunited with him on the other side. As his Lakota tradition teaches, there is no word for goodbye, only "Toksa ake," which means "We'll see you again."

Back at *Friday*, there were only more questions about how the future Wendell, Richard, and I had envisioned would play out. Even today I struggle with the irony of our shared DC experience. While I never confronted God about why he took Richard, I did say in my own mind, "God, here we were at our nation's capital, right in the middle of these reconciliation efforts, when we were just starting to get recognition for *Friday*'s work, when people were just starting to acknowledge our work on race relations, when people were just starting to at least become aware, I mean, why did you take him right then? And why did you take him in such a dramatic fashion? He died, man, at the presidential prayer breakfast!"

In an unforgettable quiet time with the Lord shortly after Richard's passing, God answered my questions. It wasn't necessarily the answer I had been expecting, or even one I wanted to hear. But it was powerful. And it has inspired me ever since.

God's message: "Richard was ready. And you're not. There's still work to be done, so go do the work."

I was like, wow! It was really kind of an unsolicited response because it was one of those things where you've just been thinking about something and never really posed it as a question. But immediately after that message I had peace about Richard. I was totally okay with the fact he was in a better place, and that God had purpose and intent for him. I still didn't understand what God was up to, but from then on I knew how to deal with the rest of the stuff that was going on around me. It was really simple. God was telling me, "Hey, look Larry, I'm specifically calling you to do something; don't try to defer or push other people up front."

Yes, it was a simple message, but I admit it has taken a lot of convincing from God to get me to fully accept there's unfinished work for me to complete. It's been a long process of me accepting the leadership role God has given me because I didn't really want it; I always felt inadequate. Now, believe me, I've got an ego, so it's not an ego problem; it's just that I was out of my element.

If it was sports, I had no problem assuming a leadership role in guiding my team to victory, which I did in most every sport I participated in since fifth grade. I may not have been the all-star, the front man who led in scoring, but I was right behind the Number One guy, gutting out win after win. I was definitely in my element on the basketball court, the baseball diamond, and the football field.

But becoming a cop, a regional spokesperson, a "racial reconciliation" guy, having anything to do with politics—those things were so far removed from my consciousness I did nothing to prepare for them. So, for God to use those life experiences as vehicles to prepare me for whatever future he has in store was totally foreign to me. I always felt like a fish out of water, always felt uncomfortable, always felt under pressure.

Looking back over my life, I acknowledge I was never the first choice for anything. Telling my future wife the first time I ever met her she would be my bride didn't endear me to Renee as her first choice for a husband. I certainly wouldn't have been Wendell's first choice for a lifelong black friend (and vice versa as I often chide my white friend for not being able to play basketball). And leading a group of blacks, whites, and Native Americans to Washington, DC, to challenge the establishment over reconciliation issues? No one in their right mind would have foreseen me as their first choice for that daunting task. I know that, even though I confess God has had to deal with my selfish and petty concerns about never being someone's first choice. But my commitment to being part of a movement where men are being redeemed, changed, and in right relationship with each other is stronger now than ever. Why? Because I'm confident my true calling is based on a promise God left me with:

"Larry, you may never be the first choice, but you'll be the right choice."

Moving Forward

I hadn't been back in a courtroom for a long time, but I wanted to be there for my friend, Ayric Payton. I had met Ayric through Larry Anderson; he's a regular at *Friday*, been part of the movement for at least ten years. Of course, as a retired criminal defense attorney I was very familiar with the inside of the courthouse. But this time I joined Ayric and his family as they sat in the audience—at the trial of his daughter's boyfriend, who was accused of murdering her.

On a Thursday, divers had discovered twenty-two-year-old Elye-sicia Payton's bludgeoned body in the Willamette River near a campsite where she and her boyfriend had been staying. The next morning Ayric was with us as we mourned the loss of his child. Larry, me, and a large contingent of our *Friday* group cried with him, prayed with him, and literally held him up in the most difficult moment of his life. But facing his daughter's murderer at his sentencing stretched Ayric to his limits. It was only because of his strong faith in God that he was able to tell the man he forgave him. Today, Ayric dedicates much of his time to mentoring younger men, like the ones from *Wednesday*, which is an offshoot of the *Friday* group. Ayric tells them he doesn't think God causes bad things to happen, but when they do God is right there with them. He said he knew this was true because every bad experience he had ever had, God didn't put him through it, he carried him through it.

Ayric's amazing story—from a teenaged gang member to a mature God-fearing husband and father—is one of hundreds of life-changing experiences I was privileged to be a part of because of my relationship with Larry. He's opened my eyes to things no one else could have ever showed me. And I can no longer unsee the truth that life in America has been very difficult for black people, primarily due to the way whites have treated them.

When he hung his badge up for good, Larry poured himself into the *Friday* movement, basically a 24/7 commitment to make himself available to men of all colors who were striving to fulfill their God-given purpose. And even though the men of *Friday* met as a group once a week, the job of developing and maintaining relationships and instructing men on their collective journey to build relationships with each other never ended. Today, he's a recognized leader of the African-American community, a man of authority whose presence is often requested at social, athletic, entertainment, and cultural affairs. And because of his more than twenty-five-year history of reaching out to the white community, he's been invited into a leadership role there, effectively integrating the monthly Portland Business Luncheon organization. One of his major accomplishments was helping secure Ambassador Andrew Young—a living icon from the civil rights era and a hero to African Americans—as the speaker at a PBL Christmas Luncheon. Larry had met the former U.S. Ambassador to the United Nations several times, and he had the honor of introducing Mr. Young at the event. I recall one of the takeaways from Mr. Young's speech that inspired Larry from a business perspective was how the former mayor of Atlanta incorporated his faith in God with his work in the business world. It was Larry's hope business people in Portland would see the benefit of intertwining the gospel with business. He just never dreamed he would be a candidate for running such an operation.

It had been tried before, but *Friday*'s track record of bringing a white man and a black man together in a business venture had a one-hundred-percent failure rate. And pretty much everyone agreed a business model where a white man deferred to a black man in charge was a sure way to create division and hostility. But what about embracing the gospel—utilizing God's Kingdom model—in a business setting, just like Mayor Young did when he turned Atlanta around? Larry reasoned a businessman's model doesn't necessarily fit with God's Kingdom model because whoever designs and makes it successful gets all the glory for making it happen. But, in Larry's and *Friday*'s spheres of influence, all the glory belongs to God. So even though Larry had had numerous business opportunities presented to him in the past, he always declined. Especially overtures from the non-profit world. He told me he even had a prepared response whenever he got asked to consider leading a non-profit organization: the only way he would ever be involved was no one could tell him what to do with the money people donated to fund the work. It was an outrageous criterion, he knew, because nobody in the non-profit sector would ever agree to do that. Until someone did.

When one of the white businessmen from *Friday* stepped up with an unfettered large donation and offered to fund whatever non-profit venture Larry desired, he couldn't resist. That's how *Friday* Group Enterprises (FGE) was born, with Larry serving as CEO. As self-labeled amateur venture capitalists, the men behind FGE hope to attract capital in order to stimulate business opportunities for people of color. The mission is not just to create more jobs, but to inspire a spirit of entrepreneurship, create businesses, and sustain those businesses. Along the way, the core group of *Friday* overseers get a front row seat to witness the machinations of business, from startups to stragglers.

I don't know if it's due to his new role as a businessman that has mellowed him out, but I think Larry's established enough now in this process that he's realized he doesn't have to always confront every issue or fight everybody all the time. I guess you could say he's okay with the fact a lot of white people are going to be white.

The world is very different—white and black. But I can't find anything in my history with Larry or with God that would say racism is right, or our separation is correct, or the way we're living is the way it should be. Just listen to the song: "Jesus loves the little children; *All* the children of the world; Red, brown, yellow, black and white..." We sing the song, but there's so little that's playing it out. Wouldn't it be nice if in our lifetime racism disappeared? But in all reality, this in an ongoing process, and it isn't going to conclude anytime soon. What's it going to be like for Larry's children and their children? That's the question.

In the end, I just hope I can be as good a friend to Larry as he has been to me. Has it been uncomfortable for me—a white man—to initiate and sustain a longtime relationship with a black man? Sure it has. But you know what, in some ways Larry is easy to love. Because he's honest. He will always be a dear friend, but I don't have any great expectations my relationship with him will have any massive impact around the world. But it's had an influence on me.

A heartfelt embrace followed Larry's introduction of me
when I spoke at a PBL Christmas Luncheon.
[Photo Credit: Diana Liz Dettwyler Photography]

WENDELL BIRKLAND was a deputy district attorney for Multnomah County for several years before starting his own criminal defense firm. He was a Sunday school teacher for more than fifteen years and remains active in groups such as Portland Business Luncheons and the National Prayer Breakfast.

LARRY ANDERSON is a former police officer with the Portland Police Bureau. He is currently the CEO of a non-profit whose aim is to attract capital and business opportunities for people of color. He is also a mentor with *Boys2Men*.

This is **KEN KOOPMAN**'s third book. He has also written *People Before Profit: The Inspiring Story of the Founder of Bob's Red Mill* (Inkwater Press, 2012); and *Kombucha Revolution: 75 Recipes for Homemade Brews, Fixers, Elixirs, and Mixers* (Ten Speed Press, 2014).

CPSIA information can be obtained
at www.ICGtesting.com
Printed in the USA
FSHW020742231218
54637FS